C. Stewart-Smith.

Hilary Staniland was born in 1941. She is at present Senior Lecturer in the Department of Religion, University of Nigeria (Nsukka campus). She has taught at the Universities of Leicester, Khartoum and York.

UNIVERSALS

Hilary Staniland

First published in the United States 1972
First published in the United Kingdom 1973
Reprinted 1978

Published by
THE MACMILLAN PRESS LTD
London and Basingstoke
Associated companies in Delhi Dublin
Hong Kong Johannesburg Lagos Melbourne
New York Singapore and Tokyo

ISBN 0 333 11076 5

Printed in Hong Kong

CONTENTS

Introduction vii

Chapter One: PLATO AND ARISTOTLE 1

Chapter Two: THE BRITISH EMPIRICISTS 28

Chapter Three: RECURRENCE AND RESEMBLANCE 53

Chapter Four: GENERAL TERMS 68

Chapter Five: LOGIC AND ONTOLOGY 84

Chapter Six: SUBJECTS AND PREDICATES 106

Suggestions for further reading 123

Bibliography 127

Index 139

INTRODUCTION

The aim of this book is to introduce the reader to the cluster of philosophical problems known as the "problem of universals." It does not itself put forward any theory of universals, nor is it in any serious sense a history of the debate. Instead, it offers sketches of a number of different approaches to the problem, as found in the work of various philosophers from Plato to the present day, in the hope of thereby putting the reader in a position to start thinking about the problem for himself. The reader should bear in mind that an outline of a philosopher's theory is not a substitute for the theory itself, and that points which seem obscure or confusing can sometimes be cleared up by consulting the original text (or, if the original text proves equally obscure, the relevant writings of other philosophers).

Questions of the kind discussed under the heading "problem of universals" arise in two areas of philosophy, ontology and the philosophy of language. Ontology is a philosophical inquiry into the question "What kinds of things are there?"

Most of us would unhesitatingly grant that there are *particulars*: everyday things such as people, horses, or tables. But are there, in addition to these, such things as the species *man*, the species *horse*, the property of *being a table*, the color *red*, or the relation *being taller than?* These latter entities (supposing them to exist, which is one of the main points in dispute) are what philosophers have called *universals*. The view that there are such entities is called "realism," or, to distinguish it from other doctrines going by the same name, the "realist theory of universals."

From the side of the philosophy of language, we have various questions arising out of the existence of *general words*. The function of the proper name "John" is to refer to some particular man of that name; likewise, the function of the phrase "the man" is to refer to some particular man. But what about the general term "man" itself? Is there anything in the real world which is the counterpart of this term, as the man John is the counterpart of the name "John"? (If so, it must presumably be a universal.) And if not, how are we to explain the role of such terms as "man" in making statements about the world?

Again, what justification have we for grouping many different things together under the same general term? Are we completely free to invent a general term for any conceivable collection of things, or must the things to which we apply the same general term satisfy some prior condition? And if they must, what is this prior condition? Is it enough to say that the things must *resemble* each other? Or must we suppose there to be some entity (again, presumably a universal) which is in some sense present in all of them, or to which they are all in some other manner related?

A recent development (though one foreshadowed by Plato) is the emergence of a version of the problem of universals in the philosophy of mathematics and of formal logic. Mathematics does not deal in universals as traditionally conceived by philosophers (though some branches of logic do), but it does deal in entities such as *numbers* and *sets*, or *classes*, which, whatever they are, are surely not particulars. And the postulation of such entities raises ontological problems of a kind very similar to those raised about universals in general philosophy.

The problem of universals is one of those philosophical problems which, to some minds, are apt to seem too abstract and technical to be of general interest. But against this two things need to be said.

First, the investigation of almost *any* philosophical problem, if taken far enough, will bring us up against some aspect of the problem of universals. So even if we do not find the problem of universals interesting in its own right, we must still recognize the need to deal with it as a means of dealing with other philosophical problems.[1]

Secondly, it is perhaps relevant to note that theories of universals have, as a matter of historical fact, been seen by philosophers as having implications of a kind to which hardly anyone could remain indifferent. In Plato, the realist theory of universals is closely associated with a sharp distinction between "the senses" and "the intellect," and an exaltation of the latter over the former. The moral and political implications of this view (or at least, what Plato took to be its implications) are clearly spelled out elsewhere in his work. We find an echo of this in Russell's *Problems of Philosophy*, where Russell suggests that the belief in real universals appeals to those who prefer perfection to life, and correspondingly fails to appeal to those who prefer life to perfection.[2]

Opponents of realism, for their part, frequently betray a certain spirit of *écrasez l'infâme*. They tend to see the doctrine they are attacking as not merely false,

[1] An illustration of this in moral philosophy is Kovesi, J., *Moral Notions* (New York, 1968).

[2] On Plato and perfection, see Passmore, J., *The Perfectibility of Man* (London, 1970), Chapter 2.

but pernicious: a web of mystification with more than a hint of sinister interests in the background. In disposing of universals and other "occult entities" they are, they feel, reasserting the claims of common sense and the plain man. There is an obvious analogy, too, between the anti-realist view of the universe as a collection of particulars and the view of society as a collection of individuals. A further source of allegiance to anti-realism is perhaps to be found in its emphasis on man's creation of the classifications in terms of which he describes the world, and his freedom to impose whatever classifications he pleases.

Whether theories of universals actually have any of these implications, or others of a similar kind, is of course another question, though one which can hardly be settled without first finding out what the theories are. Nor are the above remarks meant to imply that it is all right to believe a philosophical theory, merely because one sees in it implications for human life which are (to oneself) attractive, or that this could in itself be an argument for the truth of the theory. But it is as good a reason as any for becoming interested in a philosophical problem; pure intellectual curiosity is probably more often the result, rather than the cause, of interest in a problem.

UNIVERSALS

Chapter One

PLATO AND ARISTOTLE

Plato

The term "universal" first came into philosophy as a translation of a term used by Aristotle. But for the first treatment of the problem we have to go back further, to Plato. Plato speaks of "Forms" or "Ideas," not of "universals," but his Theory of Forms deals with the same topics which later philosophers have discussed under the heading of the "problem of universals." It may, therefore, justly be regarded as the first theory of universals.

One source of the Theory of Forms is to be found in Plato's reflections on the philosophical practice of Socrates. Socrates had been in the habit of asking such questions as "What is virtue?", "What is courage?", or "What is piety?" Questions of this form, "What is X?", may be understood in many different ways; according to context they may convey a request for almost any kind of information about X. But as Socrates intended them, such questions convey the request for a definition —the answer to the question "What is virtue?" should take the form of a definition of virtue, the answer to the question "What is courage?" should take the form of a definition of courage, and so on.

Socrates always emphasized that in asking "What is X?", he was *not* asking to be given illustrative examples of X, nor to be told what kinds of X there are. What he wanted was a general definition of the quality X, which would then serve to guide us in deciding what we ought to say about particular cases. For example, people sometimes disagree about whether a particular type of action should really be called "courageous." According to Socrates, such disputes can be settled only by first discovering the correct definition of courage. He seems, in fact, to have regarded the discovery of such definitions as a precondition of any fully rational thought.

Plato shared Socrates' belief in the importance of definition. And like Socrates, he regarded the search for definitions not as an inquiry into the way we use words, but as an inquiry into the nature of things. But he went beyond Socrates in asking himself *what kind of things* we are investigating when we seek for definitions. Are they the ordinary familiar things of everyday life, such as people, trees, or houses? Or are they entities of a different kind? It was questions such as these which led Plato to his Theory of Forms.

We have seen that, according to Socrates, the question "What is X?" cannot be answered by giving examples of X. If we are asked "What is courage?", it is no answer to give examples of actions we consider courageous; if we are asked "What is beauty?", it is no answer to give examples of things we consider beautiful. Plato accounts for this by drawing a distinction between the many things which exemplify X on the one hand, and the single entity X itself on the other. The plurality of courageous actions is to be contrasted with the single entity *courage itself;* the plurality of beautiful things is to be contrasted with the single entity *beauty itself*. When we ask "What is X?", we are inquiring about the nature of X itself. This is why a list of examples of X is no answer to our question. Most of us could produce any number of examples of things we consider beautiful; but we might go on multiplying examples indefinitely and still be in the dark as to what beauty *is*.

This line of thought provided Plato with his answer to the question "What kind of things are we investigating when we seek for definitions?" The things we are investigating are things like courage itself, beauty itself, and so forth; in other words, things of the kind which later philosophers have called "universals," and which Plato called "Forms." (The word here translated as "Form" is also sometimes translated as "Idea." But unlike the English word "idea," it does not carry the suggestion that the entity in question exists only in someone's mind.)

For Plato, the distinction between Forms and particulars marked the discovery of a whole new realm of being, a class of entities of which the ordinary unreflective man has no conscious awareness. On the basis of what has been said so far, this may seem surprising. But if we go on to look at some of the things Plato said about the Forms, we can readily understand why he saw his innovation in this light.

Plato held that the existence of the Forms is independent of the existence of particulars. Beauty itself, or the Form of Beauty (in Plato these are alternative names for the same thing), would exist whether or not there were any particular beautiful things. But particular things are beautiful only in virtue of their relation to the Form of Beauty. There is thus a relation of one-sided dependence between particulars and Forms. Particulars are what they are only in virtue of their relations to the Forms, but the Forms would be what they are even if no particulars existed at all.

Plato's reasons for holding that particulars derive their natures from Forms are fairly obvious. Beauty itself, or the Form of Beauty, is that which the many particular beautiful things share in, and in virtue of which they are beautiful. A thing which did not share in Beauty could not be beautiful.

It is less obvious why Plato should have held that Forms exist independently of particulars. Plato's argument for this position was based on the premise that there are characteristics which particular things never fully exemplify, but only approximate to. Mathematics seems to provide many examples. The geometer speaks of absolute equality or absolute circularity, but we do not find in the world around us things which are absolutely equal to one another (in length, for instance, or in volume); nor do we find things which are absolutely circular. If we examine the things closely enough, we always find some slight irregularity: the things are only *approximately* equal or circular. Other examples may be derived from ethics: it may very plausibly be argued that we never come across perfect justice or perfect goodness in the world around us.

Yet the moral philosopher may still seek to define perfect justice or perfect goodness, and the mathematician can and does define such things as absolute equality or absolute circularity. Therefore, Plato reasoned, perfect justice and the rest must be *there* to be defined. There must be Forms of perfect justice, absolute equality, and so forth, even if there are no particulars which fully exemplify these Forms.

This view of Plato's is closely connected with some of the more startling aspects of his doctrine. As we shall see later, Plato never solved to his own satisfaction the problem of characterizing the relation between particulars and the corresponding Forms, e.g., between beautiful particulars and the Form of Beauty. He was obliged to fall back on two metaphors, which continue to occur side by side throughout his work. One was the metaphor of "sharing" or "participation"—the Form is something which is somehow shared out among the particulars. The other, which is the one which concerns us here, is the metaphor of "imitation." According to this metaphor, particulars are related to Forms as imperfect copies to their originals. Beautiful particulars are poor imitations of the Form of Beauty; only the Form itself is absolutely and without qualification beautiful. And Plato held that a similar situation exists for all Forms; the related particulars are in all cases only imperfect copies.

Partly on the basis of this view, Plato maintained that Forms have a greater reality than particulars. They *are* what particulars merely strive in vain to be. Also, they have a greater reality because they are independent, eternal, and changeless, whereas particulars are dependent, transient, and in a state of continual change.

Given Plato's belief that Forms exist independently of particulars, it is not difficult to see why he held them to be eternal and changeless. Even if there were no beautiful particulars, this would not prevent the Form of Beauty from existing—and what else could prevent it from existing? So it must always exist. Again, Forms are according to Plato no more dependent on particulars for their nature than for their existence. Changes in the world of particulars do not mean changes in the Forms. And if the Form of Beauty does not change when there are changes in its related particulars, why else should it change? So it must be changeless.

The idea that the Forms are eternal and changeless was extremely important to Plato, because he held that particulars, being transient and in a state of continual change, could not be objects of genuine knowledge. Genuine knowledge for him meant knowledge of the essential natures of things, and he held that there cannot be such knowledge of a thing which is always changing, because a thing of this kind does not have any essential nature. It is no use asking what a thing really *is*, if it is liable at any moment to become something else or cease to exist altogether.

For genuine knowledge to be possible, then, there must be at least some entities which are permanent and not liable to change. Plato therefore believed that with his Theory of Forms he had found the answer to the question "How is knowledge possible, if there can be no genuine knowledge of particulars?" Knowledge is possible, because as well as particulars there are Forms, which unlike particulars are eternal and changeless. Forms, not particulars, are the objects of genuine knowledge–a conclusion which provided Plato with a further reason for holding that Forms are more real than particulars.

Knowledge of the Forms is, according to Plato, obtained by the intellect, working for the most part on information provided by the senses. Forms, unlike particulars, cannot be perceived by the senses: one cannot see or touch the Form of Beauty as one might see or touch a beautiful object. To become aware of the existence of the Forms, we have to reflect on what our senses tell us. But Plato conceived this process of reflection in a very special and peculiar way. He held that we have all had a direct intellectual perception of the Forms in a previous existence. The knowledge so obtained is forgotten at birth. But when in our ordinary existence we perceive particulars which resemble these Forms, we are reminded of our previous direct experience of the Forms and so recover our lost knowledge.[1]

Plato's argument for this theory was based on his belief in Forms which are not fully exemplified by any particulars. We can conceive of absolute equality, for

[1] This view is usually referred to as Plato's Theory of Reminiscence.

we are capable of judging that particular instances of equality fall short of it. But this awareness that there is such a thing as absolute equality is not based on any experience which we have in this life, for absolute equality does not occur in the world of particulars. So it must be based on an experience which we had in a previous life, namely that of directly perceiving the Form of Equality.

We may now sum up the main points of Plato's theory. (1) Forms, not particulars, are the subject matter of philosophical definitions of the Socratic type. (2) Particulars are dependent on Forms, but Forms are not dependent on particulars. (3) Forms are eternal and changeless, unlike particulars, which are in every case transient and in a state of continual change. (4) There can be genuine knowledge of Forms, but not of particulars. In the case of particulars, the best we may hope to achieve is true opinion. (5) Forms, unlike particulars, cannot be perceived by the senses. Only our intellect makes us aware of their existence.

We have seen that Plato saw his theory as providing an explanation of the nature of philosophical definition, and also as explaining the possibility of knowledge. In addition to this, he claimed for his theory the merit of providing a general explanation of why things are as they are–beautiful things are beautiful because they participate in the Form of the Beautiful, hot things are hot because they participate in the Form of Heat, and so on. And finally, he saw the theory as providing a justification for the use of general words. Different things may be called by the same name, because different things may participate in the same Form.

Criticism of the Theory of Forms may conveniently be left until after we have considered the views of Aristotle, in whose work we shall find many of the most serious objections to Plato's theory being raised.

Aristotle

Aristotle is generally classified along with Plato as a realist. But his realism was of a very different kind from Plato's. Indeed, one could easily get the impression from his explicit comments on Plato that there was no common ground between the two philosophers at all.

The central point in Aristotle's criticism of Plato concerns Plato's belief in the "separate existence" of the Forms. According to Plato, as we have seen, there is a relation of one-sided dependence between Forms and particulars: particulars depend for their existence on Forms, but Forms do not in the same way depend on particulars. The Forms thus exist separately, in the sense that one could remove the particulars, and the Forms would still be there.

Aristotle entirely rejects this view. For him, it is no more possible for universals to exist without particulars than it is for particulars to exist without universals. And he conceives the impossibility as being of the same order as that of a smile existing without a face. A smile simply *is* something which appears on a face, and likewise, *man* simply *is* a species to which particular individuals belong. It is essential to the nature of universals to be related to particulars; we should not conceive of this relation as something added onto a separately existing entity. And this is exactly what Plato did. The Platonic Form is a universal conceived of as capable of existing on its own, independently of any relation to particulars, and is therefore according to Aristotle an impossible entity.

Aristotle also makes what is essentially the same point by saying that Plato, in his view mistakenly, took universals to be *substances*. We need therefore to consider what Aristotle meant by "substance."

In the *Categories*, Aristotle explains the term "substance" by making use of two further technical terms: "being in" and "being said of." "Being in" (in this particular context) is used by Aristotle to indicate a certain relation of one-sided dependence which may exist between two particulars. The example of the smile and the face which was used above may serve as an example of this: the smile cannot exist without the face, but the face can very well exist without the smile. In Aristotle's terminology, then, the smile is "in" the face.

"Being said of," on the other hand, indicates a relation between a universal and a particular: thus the universal *man* or the universal *wise* is "said of" the particular, Socrates. One might imagine that Aristotle is speaking here of the relation between the *word* "man" and the particulars it is applied to, but this is not the case: "being said of" is intended to be understood as a relation between things, not between a word and a thing. What Aristotle has in mind, then, is the relation which the universal *man* has to a particular thing if it is true that the particular thing is a man.

As already indicated, the "being said of" relation also involves a certain kind of dependence. Clearly the universal *man* does not depend for its existence on the existence of Socrates as such, or any other particular man as such, but it does depend for its existence on the existence of some particular man or other. This is so because *man*, being a universal, is the kind of entity which exists only in being "said of" something, and hence can exist only if some particular man exists whom it is "said of."

Having made clear what he means by "being in" and "being said of," Aristotle goes on to explain the term "substance." Substances, he says, are those things which are neither "in" anything nor "said of" anything, and he gives as examples of substances a particular man or a particular horse.

Thus when Aristotle says that Plato mistakenly regarded universals as substances, this turns out to be basically no more than another way of saying that he mistakenly regarded universals as capable of existing separately from particulars. For what Aristotle is suggesting is that Plato may be thought of as assimilating universals to those things which are neither "in" anything nor "said of" anything. But if Plato did this, he was not, from Aristotle's point of view, wrong in denying that universals exist "in" anything, for Aristotle too holds that universals do not exist "in" anything. So Plato's error must have lain in denying that universals are "said of" anything. And, given the nature of Aristotle's explanation of the term "said of," the only point which Plato could reasonably be interpreted as having denied is Aristotle's claim that a universal has to be "said of" something in order to exist. And this of course he would have denied.

However, Aristotle's meaning in saying that Plato took universals to be substances may also be brought out in a slightly different way. Aristotle clearly thought that Plato believed universals to be more similar to the things which he, Aristotle, classified as substances (e.g., particular men or horses) than they really are. This may seem surprising when Plato was at such pains to emphasize the differences between Forms and particulars. But there is one element of his theory which fully bears out Aristotle's view, namely the doctrine of imitation. Plato sometimes speaks of particulars as copies or imitations of the Forms, and in line with this, he holds that the Form of the Beautiful, for example, is itself beautiful. And we may readily agree with Aristotle that Plato is here treating universals and particulars as alike in a way in which they could not possibly be alike. At this point in his theory, Plato does really seem to be thinking of the Form as though it were merely a particular of a very peculiar kind.

We also find that when Plato talks in a general way about definition, he is apt to give the impression that definition is a matter of describing an individual object—though of course an individual object of a special kind, namely a Form. (The actual definitions which Plato puts up for discussion in various places do not sound in the least like descriptions of individual objects, but that is another matter.) Aristotle therefore puts forward as an objection to Plato the argument that the Forms cannot be the objects of definition, because the Forms are individuals and there cannot be any definition of an individual. The reason he gives for this view is that to define an individual we would have to produce a set of characteristics which necessarily belonged only to that one individual and could not belong to any other, and this cannot be done.

So when Aristotle says that Plato treats universals as substances, he is making two points: he is saying that Plato regards them as capable of existing independently of particulars, and also that Plato fails to grasp the really basic difference between universals and particulars (namely, that a universal is an entity which is "said of" something, whereas a particular is not), and hence tends to think of universals as if they were particulars of a peculiar kind.

To return now to Aristotle's own views. In the passage from the *Categories* to which I have been referring, Aristotle distinguishes three main kinds of entity: those which are "in" something but are not "said of" anything (e.g., a smile), those which are "said of" something but are not "in" anything (universals), and those which are neither "in" anything nor "said of" anything (substances). (Aristotle also mentions a further class of entities which are both "in" something and "said of" something, but this is a complication which need not concern us here.)

Aristotle goes on to say that everything which exists is either a substance, or "in" a substance, or "said of" a substance. Therefore, he concludes, if substances did not exist, nothing could exist; a conclusion which clearly brings out the way in which he regards both "being in" and "being said of" as involving dependence.

One might get the impression here that Aristotle's view is the direct opposite of Plato's: instead of self-sufficient Forms and dependent particulars, self-sufficient, particular substances and dependent universals. In fact, however, Aristotle does not regard particular substances as self-sufficient in the sense in which Plato regarded the Forms as self-sufficient. For Plato, the world of Forms would still exist even if there were no particulars at all. But Aristotle does not hold that particular substances could exist even if there were no universals at all.

We can easily see why he could not hold this. One cannot conceive of a particular substance existing without at the same time being a thing of some specific kind and having certain specific characteristics. And on a realist view such as Aristotle's, to say this is to say that the particular substance could not exist unless certain universals existed also.

It is true that this argument does not show that the existence of a particular substance requires the existence of any *one* universal; but then, the existence of a universal does not require the existence of any *one* particular substance either. And Aristotle in fact holds that in one special kind of case, the existence of a particular substance *does* require the existence not just of some universal or other, but of a specific universal.

This occurs when the universal is of the kind which Aristotle calls "secondary substances."

So far, I have represented Aristotle as applying the term "substance" only to particular objects such as men or horses. This is correct insofar as Aristotle regards this as the basic and primary sense of the term. But as just indicated, he also holds that certain universals may be called "substances" in a secondary sense. "Substance" therefore includes both particular substances such as men and horses ("primary" substances), and also certain universals ("secondary" substances).

The universals which Aristotle calls secondary substances are those which tell us *what a thing is,* what *kind* it is, e.g., "man," "horse," or "tree." The distinction which Aristotle has in mind here is not merely a grammatical one, such as the distinction in English between common nouns and adjectives, although we shall normally find that words of the secondary substance type are indicated by common nouns. "This is a man," would, for Aristotle, count as an answer to the question "What is this?", whereas "This is white" would not. Here "man" is, in English, a noun, and "white" an adjective. But equally, "This is human" would count as an answer, whereas "This is a white thing" would not, although here the grammatical position is reversed. So we should not confuse Aristotle's distinction with the distinction in English grammar between common nouns and adjectives.

The idea Aristotle is working with, when he speaks of secondary substance, is that we can ask of any primary substance *what* it is, as opposed to asking, for example, what it is like or how it is related to other things. We cannot strictly say that there will be only one true answer to this question in each case, for the question may be answered on different levels of generality: we may truly say of one and the same thing "This is a man," "This is an animal," or "This is a living creature." So what we actually have is a series of possible answers of increasing generality, such that once the first and most specific answer is given, the rest follow of necessity—(if this is a man, then it *must* be an animal). And each of the universals mentioned in this series of answers will fall under the heading of secondary substance.

Because secondary substance gives us *what a thing is*, it stands in a peculiarly intimate relation to the particular substance. One can conceive of Socrates without his wisdom or without his paunch, but one cannot conceive of Socrates without his humanity, for Socrates *is* a man, and so if you take away the humanity, you take away Socrates. (Likewise, and for the same reasons, one cannot conceive of Socrates not being an animal.) Hence, the existence of a primary substance always requires the existence of a certain specific secondary substance. If there was no such species as *man*, there could not be such an individual as Socrates.

This doctrine of secondary substance is closely connected with Aristotle's views on definition and classification. Definition, for Aristotle, is always definition of universals, and, more especially, of secondary substances. And defining a secondary substance he conceives as a matter of fitting it into a certain scheme of classification. Thus if we want to define the species *man*, we need to know on the one hand what kind of things men are (the genus of the species), and on the other what distinguishes them from other things of this kind (the differentia of the species). So one might for instance explain what men are by saying that the species *man* belongs to the genus *animal*, and is differentiated from other species of this genus by the possession of *rationality*.

Definition is thus carried out in relation to a system

of classification according to which things are divided into various kinds (genera), which in turn are divided into various sub-kinds (species), these being distinguished from each other by certain characteristic properties (differentia). "Genus" and "species" are relative terms: *animal* is a genus relative to *man*, but a species relative to *living creature*. There is thus a hierarchy of classes: a given class A may be divided into the species B, C, and D, of which B may be divided into E, F, and G, C into H, I, and J, and so on.

Aristotle holds not only that this system of genera, species, and differentia is the only truly scientific method of classification, but also that, as applied to any given subject matter, the method can yield only *one* correct result. There could not, for instance, be two different but equally acceptable ways of classifying plants into genera and species. Either such a system of classification reflects the order of things in nature, in which case it is correct, or it does not, in which case it is incorrect.

Consideration of the views of Plato and Aristotle

Plato and Aristotle are both realists in the sense of holding that the world contains universals as well as particulars. But they differ sharply in their views of what universals are and how they are related to particulars. For Plato, universals, or in his own terminology Forms, are self-sufficient entities which may or may not have particulars related to them. For Aristotle, universals exist only in virtue of their relation to particulars, and it is only in terms of this relation that we can even explain what a universal is.

The most obvious consequence of adopting an Aristotelian form of realism, as opposed to a Platonic one, is that on an Aristotelian view there is no room for universals corresponding to general terms which do not in fact apply to anything. If we follow Aristotle, we shall have to say that there is a universal man, but there is not, for instance, a universal *centaur*, since there are not any centaurs for such a universal to be "said of." In Plato's theory, on the other hand, there is nothing to prevent us from postulating such a universal.

It has sometimes been suggested that this is a *prima facie* argument in favor of a Platonic form of realism, on the ground that there certainly are meaningful general terms which do not apply to anything, and every meaningful general term ought to have a universal corresponding to it. And clearly if we accept both of these assumptions, we shall have to allow for universals which do not have any particulars related to them, and shall therefore have to reject the Aristotelian type of realism.

Modern writers who have argued that there must be a universal for every meaningful general term have sometimes done so on the ground that words can have meaning only by standing for something, and since a general term plainly does not stand for a particular, it must stand for a universal instead. It is therefore relevant to notice that neither Plato nor Aristotle bases his realism on an argument of this kind. Aristotle does in fact allow for the possibility of general terms which do not apply to anything, and therefore cannot according to his theory stand for universals. And Plato, though he seems finally to have inclined to the view that there is a Form for every general term, did not regard this as by any means obvious. On the contrary, we find him raising such questions as whether there are Forms of man-made objects, or of things like hair or dirt. The existence of such Forms was far less evident to him than the existence of moral and mathematical Forms. So whatever his final conclusions, he certainly did not *start* from the assumption that every meaningful general term has its corresponding Form.

I do not wish to raise here the question what direct arguments might be advanced for the view that every meaningful general term must stand for a universal. As we have just seen, neither Plato nor Aristotle derives his realism from such a view of meaning. The question I do wish to raise is whether there is any kind of inconsistency in holding a realist theory of universals, and at the same time maintaining that certain general terms have no universal corresponding to them.

One might think of arguing as follows. If we can give a full and adequate account of the meaning of general terms without needing to bring in universals, the main reason for postulating universals at all disappears. Now if there are any general terms to which no universals correspond, it must be in principle possible to give an account of at least these terms without bringing in universals. But there is no significant difference between, say, "man" and "centaur," considered simply as words; both are general terms in exactly the same sense, and have meaning in exactly the same way. So if we can explain how "centaur" functions without bringing in universals, we can do the same for "man." Hence *all* general terms can be accounted for without bringing in universals.

However, there are several flaws in this argument. For one thing, it is far from clear that the case for a realist theory of universals must be based on the argument that universals need to be postulated in order to explain the working of general words. We have already seen that with Plato this argument plays only a subsidiary role. What he is chiefly concerned to explain is not the working of general words as such, but philosophical definition, the possibility of knowledge, and the characteristics of particular things. Even if we reject all these arguments in the form in which Plato propounded them, we should still leave open the possibility that other arguments for a realist view might be found which are not based on the need to explain the working of general words.

More subtly, we may question whether the case for realism needs to be of this kind at all. Need the realist argue that there must be universals, because without assuming universals such and such things can't be explained? After all, we do not–at least, not until we have been influenced by post-Cartesian philosophy–assume that the existence of particular physical objects needs to be proved in this kind of way. And perhaps a realist might argue that the existence of universals does not need to be proved in this kind of way either.

Secondly, we should not too hastily assume that if there are general terms to which no universal corresponds, the working of these general terms can be explained without bringing in universals at all. The most we can say is that if we succeeded in giving an account of such general terms, we *might* find that our account made no use of universals. But we cannot simply assume this in advance. It is equally possible that we might find, say, that though the use of a term such as "centaur" could be explained without bringing in a universal *centaur*, it could not be explained without bringing in the universals *man* and *horse*. In other words, general terms lacking a corresponding universal might be possible only against a background of general terms for which there are corresponding universals.

Thirdly, though this point is in a way implied by the previous one, it is disputable whether a term like "centaur" and a term like "man" really can be accounted for in exactly the same way. Our understanding of the term "centaur" seems to be dependent on our understanding of "man" and "horse," in a way in which our understanding of "man" is not dependent on our understanding of any other terms. And if this is so, perhaps an adequate theory of meaning could not give an account of "centaur" strictly parallel to that of "man."

We may conclude, therefore, that the argument put forward above does not as it stands succeed in establishing that a realist theory has to be based on the assumption that there is a universal for every general term. So we have not yet seen reason to reject the possibility of a tenable realistic theory which, like Aristotle's, implies that where a general term does not apply to anything, there is no corresponding universal.

Another objection which might be advanced against such a theory is that if there is no universal where the general term does not apply to anything, a universal may in certain circumstances cease to exist, or in certain other circumstances begin to exist. For example, if the horse became extinct, then presumably the universal horse would cease to exist. And we may feel with Plato that universals are not the kind of things which can begin to exist or cease to exist.

This is a very strong objection if we assume that a general term has meaning only when there is a universal corresponding to it, for we shall then be obliged to say that if the horse became extinct, the word "horse" would become meaningless, which is absurd. But if we do not make this assumption, the force of the objection is less clear. It is perhaps not particularly natural to say that the color red would cease to exist if there was no longer anything red in the world, but it is not particularly natural either to say that it would continue to exist, unless this means simply that the word "red" would still have a meaning. And if we wouldn't say "red has ceased to exist" in such circumstances, the reason could simply be that we don't need this expression because we can say "there are no longer any red things" instead.

An objection which Plato himself would have raised to the idea that where a general term does not apply to anything, there is no corresponding universal, is the following. Both Plato and Aristotle believed in the possibility of what has come to be called "real definition" —that is to say, definition of *things* as opposed to *words*. Now Plato would have argued that we could still seek to define courage, for example, even if there were no courageous men. And what we would be looking for would be a real definition, a definition of the thing courage, not of the word. So the thing courage, or in Plato's terminology the Form of Courage, must be there to be defined whether or not there are any courageous men.

There are two possible ways in which one might oppose Plato here. One might argue that although there is such a thing as real definition, there cannot be real definition in the sort of case in question here. Aristotle, for example, would have said that although we can give a real definition of man, we certainly cannot give a real definition of centaur, and when we consider how Aristotle conceived definition this seems entirely reasonable. We would not think of demanding that a biologist should find a place for centaurs in his system of classification, which is roughly what an Aristotelian "real definition" of centaur would amount to.

On the other hand one might argue, as most contemporary philosophers would, that Plato's argument fails because there is no such thing as real definition at all. Words can be defined, but things cannot. The case against real definition cannot be expounded here, but the following point may be worth making.

Much of the plausibility of the idea of real definition comes from the fact that often when we seek to define something, we are aware that we are struggling to meet some requirement which is not merely that of conforming to ordinary usage—for example, when we ask ourselves "What is freedom?" or "What is democracy?" Now it is very easy to assume that this requirement is the requirement of describing something, freedom or democracy or whatever, as it really is. But in fact many alternative explanations are available. We may be trying to express clearly a rather vague idea in our minds, or trying to find a definition which will prove useful for certain specific purposes, or, for that matter, a definition which will suit our own prejudices. All these are requirements other than the simple requirement of conforming to actual usage, but none of them need imply that we are trying to define a thing rather than a word. And once this is realized, the idea of real definition becomes far less persuasive.

This discussion started from the question whether it is an objection to Aristotelian realism, as opposed to Platonic realism, that it does not leave room for universals corresponding to general terms which do not apply to anything. But we have not discovered any convincing argument against ruling out such universals. However, this is not in itself an argument in favor of the Aristotelian type of realism, and we must therefore go on to consider what further reasons might be put forward for preferring one type of realism to the other.

I think one may safely say that most people, confronted with Plato's views and Aristotle's, would feel that the views of Aristotle are much closer to common sense. And this reaction is in a way supported by the attitudes of the two philosophers themselves. Plato is the kind of realist who sees himself as bringing news of a realm of entities of which the ordinary man is only dimly aware, if indeed he is aware of them at all.

Aristotle, by contrast, is the kind of realist who is inclined to regard the existence of universals as simply obvious. Plato definitely tries to prove the existence of the Forms, but Aristotle does not in the same way try to prove the existence of universals—he is much more concerned to prove the non-existence of Plato's Forms.

We feel that Aristotle's views are closer to common sense because in Plato's theory both the Forms and their relation to particulars are apt to seem puzzling and mysterious, while Aristotle's universals seem to be easily identifiable with familiar things such as colors, biological species, and the like. But is this impression well-founded?

Much of the immediate plausibility of Aristotle's theory comes from the fact that his talk about universals can very easily be read as a restatement in philosophical language of very ordinary and familiar facts. When Aristotle says that the universal *man* is "said of" Socrates, or that the universal *white* is "said of" such and such an object, he does not seem to be claiming to tell us anything we did not know already when we judged that Socrates was a man or that the object was white. But when Plato tells us that men are men in virtue of their relation to the Form of Man, or that beautiful things are beautiful in virtue of their relation to the Form of Beauty, he definitely does claim to be telling us something new. And the puzzle is to understand what this new information can possibly be. What on earth is "imitating" or "participating" in the Form of Beauty, if it is not the same thing as just being beautiful? Plato himself was seriously concerned about this problem. In one of his later dialogues, the *Parmenides*, he advances arguments attacking his own theory at precisely this point, and it has even been maintained by some commentators that toward the end of his life he abandoned the Theory of Forms because of these very difficulties. The two most important arguments in the *Parmenides* are directed against the metaphors of "imitation" and "participation" respectively.

The argument against the metaphor of "imitation" is as follows. According to the "imitation" version of the Theory of Forms, the resemblance between particular beautiful things, in virtue of which we call them all "beautiful," can be made intelligible only by postulating a Form of Beauty which all the particular beautiful things resemble. But if the first resemblance really stands in need of an explanation of this kind, surely the second resemblance does too. So in order to make the resemblance between particular beautiful things and the Form of Beauty intelligible, we shall have to postulate a second Form which all the particular beautiful things *and* the Form of Beauty resemble, and so on ad infinitum. At each stage we still have an unexplained resemblance on our hands, and so the explanation can never be completed. This sort of difficulty is inevitable if we assume on the one hand that resemblances, as such, stand in need of explanation, and on the other that they can be explained only in terms of further resemblances. (Plato himself does not use the example of the Form of Beauty, but simply states the argument in general terms. Later, the Form of Man came to be the standard example, and the argument is therefore traditionally known as the "Third Man Argument.")[2]

The kind of difficulties Plato found himself in with the alternative metaphor of "participation" may be brought out as follows. The idea here is that the Form is somehow *shared in* by the particulars. Each beautiful

[2] The "Third Man Argument" is an example of what are now called "infinite regress" arguments. See the chapter on infinite regress arguments in Passmore, J., *Philosophical Reasoning* (New York, 1961).

thing has a share of Beauty, each human being a share of Humanity, and so on. The difficulty here is as follows. Are we to think of the particulars as sharing in the Form in the way that several people might share a cake? Then the Form will be divided into separate parts belonging to different particulars. But then we have to explain how it is that all these separate parts nevertheless constitute *one* thing. So we have merely replaced the problem of explaining why this beautiful thing and that may both be called by the same name by the problem of explaining why the beauty of this thing and the beauty of that thing may both be called parts of the same Form, which is hardly an advance.

Should we say, then, that the *whole* Form is present in each of the particulars? Then we shall have to say that the Form is in many separate places at the same time. And even if we do not disallow this as absurd, we shall still have to explain how "Beauty" can be the name both of what is to be found in this thing and of what is to be found in that thing. So again, we have only replaced one problem by another.

Such difficulties as these suggest that perhaps Plato set himself an impossible problem. If we refuse to allow "This thing participates in (or imitates) the Form of Beauty" to mean the same as "This thing is beautiful," we thereby deprive ourselves of the possibility of giving any adequate account of its meaning. But must Plato refuse to allow this?

The answer is that he certainly must, if the Theory of Forms is to have the kind of explanatory force which he intended it to have. Plato wanted to explain the characteristics of particulars by saying, for instance, that beautiful things are beautiful *because* of their relation to Beauty, and he also wanted to justify the use of general terms by saying that beautiful things are called "beautiful" *because* of their relation to beauty.

Thus for Plato, the statement "these things are all called 'beautiful' in virtue of their relation to Beauty" should be compared not to a trivial statement such as "These men are all called 'Robinson' because they are all Robinsons," but to a genuinely explanatory statement such as "These men are all called 'Robinson' because they are all Robinson's sons." Likewise, the statement "These things are beautiful because of their relation to Beauty" should be compared not to the statement "These men are noblemen because they are noblemen," but to the statement "These men are noblemen because they are the sons of a nobleman."

But the statement "These men are all called 'Robinson' because they are all Robinson's sons" is explanatory precisely because "being called Robinson" does *not* mean the same as "being the son of Robinson." And likewise, "These men are noblemen because they are the sons of a nobleman" is genuinely explanatory because "being a nobleman" does *not* mean the same as "being the son of a nobleman." So if Plato's statements about the relation of particulars to Forms are to be construed on this model, it is absolutely essential that "participating in Beauty" (or "imitating Beauty") should mean something *different* from "being beautiful." And it is this requirement which got Plato into such difficulties.

Whether Plato could have avoided these difficulties, even at the price of abandoning the explanatory claims he makes for the Theory of Forms, is a further question. If Plato, like Aristotle, had started from our understanding of subject-predicate sentences such as "Socrates is a man" or "This object is white" and explained the Forms in terms of this, we would have been making the relation between Forms and particulars an integral part of his account of what the Forms are. And it is difficult to see how this could be reconciled with the conception of the Forms as independently existing entities.

We find, therefore, that realism of the Platonic type runs into difficulties of a kind which do not exist for realism of the Aristotelian type. And we have not found any positive advantages for Platonic realism to offset this. The virtues, or otherwise, of Aristotelian realism as opposed to the various kinds of anti-realism are of course another matter.

Conceptualism and Nominalism

In view of their relatively slight influence on modern philosophy, the contributions of medieval philosophers to the debate on universals will not be discussed here. However, there is one important respect in which the medieval philosophers did strongly influence the course of subsequent work on universals. The division of theories of universals into *realist*, *conceptualist*, and *nominalist* theories dates from this period, and has remained influential ever since.

Realist theories, as we have already seen, are those according to which general words (or at any rate, *some* general words) correspond to "real universals," thought of as entities existing independently of the human mind. *Conceptualist* theories attempt to dispense with real universals by instead relating general words to *concepts* or *general ideas*. The theory of Locke, discussed in the following chapter, is an example of such a theory. *Nominalist* theories attempt to explain the use of general words without depending on either the real universals of the realist or the general ideas of the conceptualist.

In this book, I have used the term "extreme nominalism" to refer to that form of nominalism which regards the calling of many things by the same name as the result of an act of arbitrary choice. This cannot be assumed to be the only possible form of nominalism, for a nominalist might hold that the use of general words is in some sense governed by principles, but deny that these principles need to be accounted for in terms of real universals or general ideas. For some purposes, the differences between conceptualist and nominalist theories matter less than their common rejection of real universals. I have therefore sometimes used the term "anti-realist" to cover conceptualist and nominalist theories alike.

Chapter Two

THE BRITISH EMPIRICISTS

How the British Empiricist philosophers conceived the problem of universals is clearly brought out by the following words of Locke: "Since all things that exist are merely particulars, how come we by general terms?"[1] For Locke, as for his successors Berkeley and Hume, the problem is to explain the use of general terms in a manner compatible with there being nothing in the world but particulars.

We do not find any of these philosophers arguing directly for the proposition that nothing exists except particulars. Rather, it is among their basic philosophical assumptions. But in defense of this assumption, it is necessary for them to show that it does not rule out a satisfactory account of general terms. If this can be done, these philosophers think, the case against universals may be taken as established: they do not envisage the possibility of there being strong arguments for the existence of universals which would not be demolished by showing that general terms can be adequately explained without them. Giving a suitable account of general terms therefore becomes the key problem.

Before going on to see how they tackled this problem, we should briefly consider the philosophical background which made it natural for Locke, Berkeley, and Hume

[1] *Essay Concerning Human Understanding,* "Of General Terms," 6.

to assume that only particulars exist. The basic idea of their empiricism is that all knowledge comes from experience, experience being taken to consist of sense perception on the one hand, and reflection or introspection on the other. For such a view, any kind of entity or alleged entity which is not an immediate object of experience poses a problem: how can we know that such entities exist, or know anything about them, if we cannot directly perceive them?

Now for the British Empiricists, the immediate objects of experience are certain entities called "ideas" (or in Hume, "ideas" and "impressions"). This word cannot be taken quite in its ordinary sense: it is a semi-technical term deliberately introduced to stand for whatever entities are the immediate objects of experience. There is some difficulty involved in determining just what sort of entities these immediate objects of experience are supposed to be, especially in the case of Locke. But it is quite plain that whatever "ideas" are, they are not to be identified with ordinary physical objects, or at any rate, not with ordinary physical objects as we normally conceive of them. And it is these "ideas" which are taken to be the only unproblematic entities, unproblematic because they are the only things which can be directly perceived. All other kinds of entity, including physical objects and minds, constitute a problem: either some special explanation must be given to account for our knowledge of them, or their existence must be denied altogether.

From this point of view, universals could only be among the entities whose existence or supposed existence poses a problem. Those philosophers who had asserted the existence of universals had always maintained that universals could not be directly perceived by the senses, and that our knowledge of them therefore depends on the intellect. Furthermore—and this is the crucial point—none of the philosophers we are considering would have classed universals along with physical objects and minds as entities whose existence the ordinary man takes for granted. As they saw it, universals are strictly philosopher's entities, creations of theory which no one in the course of his everyday life ever has occasion to think about. The problems posed by physical objects or minds could not be disposed of outright by simply asserting that no such things exist, for this would do violence to common sense. But in the case of universals, they thought, such a course could be taken without doing violence to anything except obscure and outdated philosophical theories. It is therefore not surprising that it seemed the obvious course to take.

There is a certain historical oddity in this situation. The scholastic philosophy which the British Empiricists were opposing was ultimately derived from Aristotle, by way of medieval realism. And the writings of Aristotle himself do not leave one with the impression that universals are mysterious entities somehow hidden behind the visible phenomena of everyday life. Nevertheless, this is how the British Empiricists saw the universals of the scholastic philosophers of their time, no doubt with some justice. And when they thought of universals, it was universals so conceived which they were thinking of. They would probably have thought it simply perverse if anyone had supposed that by speaking of colors and shapes, for instance, they might be tacitly acknowledging the existence of universals. For colors and shapes, surely, are not "occult entities"—there is nothing hidden or mysterious about them.

This, then, was the background against which it seemed reasonable to assert, almost as a matter of course, that "everything which exists is only a particular." We must now look at the way in which these philosophers set about the task of providing an account of general terms which should be consistent with this position.

The role of "ideas" as the immediate objects of experience has already been touched on. These "ideas" include both what is immediately present to the mind in sense perception and what is immediately present to the mind in thinking or imagining. (In Hume, only the latter are called "ideas"—the former he calls "impressions.") In addition to their epistemological role, ideas also play a central role in the British Empiricists' approach to the problem of meaning. Words are seen as having meaning insofar as they stand for ideas.

So we find Locke introducing the topic of meaning thus: "The use of words is to be sensible marks of ideas, and the ideas they stand for are their proper and immediate signification. The use men have of these marks being either to record their own thoughts for the assistance of their own memory; or, as it were, to bring out their ideas, and lay them before the view of others: words in their primary and immediate signification stand for nothing, *but the ideas in the mind of him that uses them*."[2]

Since the function of words is to stand for ideas, the problem about general terms is seen as turning on the question "In what sense, if any, are there *general ideas?*" That is, should we suppose that just as there are both singular terms and general terms, so there are also both particular ideas and general ideas, the singular terms standing for particular ideas and the general terms for general ideas? And if there are general ideas, what is it that distinguishes them from particular ideas—is it something intrinsic to the ideas themselves, or merely the use to which they are put in thought? These are the

[2] *Essay Concerning Human Understanding*, "Of the Signification of Words," 1–2.

questions to which we shall find Locke, Berkeley, and Hume applying themselves.

Locke

Locke's view is that there are indeed general ideas, and that the special characteristic which distinguishes them from particular ideas is their being arrived at by a process of *abstraction*. We accordingly find Locke referring to these same ideas as "abstract" or "abstract general" ideas.

In asserting that there are general ideas as well as particular ideas, Locke is at pains to emphasize that even general ideas are, as he puts it, "particular in their existence." Locke's purpose here is to avoid any confusions which might arise from the ambiguity of the phrase "particular idea." "Particular idea," as used by Locke, means "idea of a particular," e.g., my idea of the moon. But it might in a different context be taken to mean "idea which *is* a particular." And the point Locke is making is simply that all ideas *are* particulars, whether or not they are also *of* particulars.

General terms, according to Locke, get their meaning by being made to stand for general ideas. And these general ideas are created by the mind by a process of abstraction. This phrase, "created by the mind," is crucial to Locke's theory. To appreciate its significance, we must consider it in relation to the distinction Locke makes between *simple* and *complex* ideas.

Locke's account of simple ideas is at many points confused and ambiguous, and has therefore always given rise to difficulties of interpretation. But for our purposes the main points are these. Simple ideas, as Locke defines them, are ideas which are not compounds of other ideas. Locke holds that in its perception of simple ideas the mind is wholly passive. We know only those simple ideas which experience provides us with, and cannot ourselves invent any new ones. But with complex ideas the position is different. For instance, we may have the idea of centaur, although experience has not provided any of us with this idea, no one having actually perceived a centaur. This is possible because "centaur" is a complex idea. We can form the idea without having perceived a centaur, because we can ourselves create it out of the ideas of man and horse. It is in this sense that complex ideas, unlike simple ones, can be created by the mind.

Abstraction, as Locke conceives it, is one of the chief processes by means of which the mind forms complex ideas out of other ideas, and ultimately out of simple ideas. General ideas therefore fall into the class of complex ideas. And as with all complex ideas, there is no need for the idea to be actually given in experience. We have seen that we can have the idea of centaur without having actually perceived a centaur. But a similar though more subtle point can be made of the idea of centaur and the idea of man alike. We have none of us actually perceived *man;* we have only perceived particular men. Hence the general idea of man is not the idea of anything we have actually perceived, in the sense in which my idea of a friend's face is the idea of something I have actually perceived.

The importance of the claim that general ideas are created by the mind should by now be clear. To the experience of merely imagining my friend's face there corresponds the experience of actually seeing his face. But there is no experience which in a similar way corresponds to the experience of thinking of man as such. And it is essential to Locke's theory that there should not be, for then there would have to be a universal *man* to be the object of this experience.

Let us see now how Locke conceives the process of abstraction. As we have seen in the example of the idea of centaur, some general ideas are created out of other already existing general ideas. This must be so when, as in the case of the idea of centaur, there does not in fact exist anything falling under that idea. And it may be so even in other cases, e.g., if I acquire the idea of zebra not by seeing zebras, but by reading descriptions of them. But the fundamental process in the creation of general ideas is the process of abstraction by means of which we create the general ideas out of the ideas provided by experience of particular things falling under that idea. If we did not have the power to create general ideas in this way, we would not be in a position to create further general ideas such as that of centaur from the general ideas we already have.

Locke introduces the term "abstraction" as follows: "The mind makes the particular ideas, received from particular objects, to become general; which is done by considering them as they are in the mind such appearances, separate from all other existences and the circumstances of real existence, as time, place or any other concomitant ideas. This is called *abstraction*. . . ."[3] Thus, to use Locke's own example, we observe the whiteness of a piece of paper, the whiteness of some snow, the whiteness of some milk, and so on, and by separating out the whiteness from the other accompanying ideas (e.g., the flatness of the paper or the coldness of the snow) we form the general idea of *white*.

This account as it stands has two dubious features which Locke himself modifies elsewhere. The first is that Locke seems to be talking as though the idea of whiteness which we receive from the paper is the *same*

[3] *Essay Concerning Human Understanding*, "Of Discerning," 9.

idea as that which we receive from the snow. And this can hardly be reconciled with Locke's insistence that ideas are particulars. If ideas are particulars, we cannot literally receive the same idea on one occasion from a piece of paper and on another from a piece of snow, for then we would be encountering two instances of the same idea, and particulars, unlike universals, are not supposed to have instances. One may, from a realist point of view, speak of instances of the universal *man*, but one may not speak of instances of the particular Socrates. To be consistent with his own presuppositions, therefore, the most Locke can claim is that the idea we receive from the paper and the idea we receive from the snow are two *similar* ideas. We accordingly find that in his further development of the theory, Locke speaks of abstraction as based on the observation of similarities, rather than on the encountering of one and the same idea on different occasions. Even here, however, it is doubtful whether Locke appreciates the full force of the difficulty.

The other misleading feature of the account of abstraction quoted above is its failure to bring out the point that the idea obtained by this process is one which could never have been given to us in experience. One might easily imagine Locke to be saying that when we perceive a particular man, for example, we receive the idea of man along with a bundle of others, which we then discard to get the idea of man in its pure form. And this is not what he wants to say, for according to his theory we never receive the idea of man as such from experience at all.

So abstraction cannot simply be a matter of picking out from a bundle of ideas the one we are interested in. But if it is not this, what is it?

Locke's own awareness of this difficulty comes out in the much-discussed passage about the idea of triangle. He says: ". . . Does it not require some pains and skill to form the general idea of a triangle? . . . For it must be neither oblique nor rectangle, neither equilateral, equicrural nor scalenon; but all and none of these at once. In effect, it is something imperfect, that cannot exist; an idea wherein some parts of several different and inconsistent ideas are put together."[4]

Locke's way of expressing himself here is obscure, not to say perverse. On the face of it he is saying, first, that the general idea of triangle has inconsistent properties, and secondly, that it does not exist. And yet it is not impossible to have such an idea, merely difficult. Clearly we cannot take him quite literally. The passage is perhaps best taken as expressing an unresolved conflict in Locke's mind between the inclination to say that forming the general idea of triangle is the same thing as forming the idea of a triangle which has *no* properties except its triangularity, and the recognition that this can't be right, because such a triangle is inconceivable.

Underlying this dilemma is Locke's tendency to think of ideas as mental pictures. Abstraction then becomes like a process of taking the picture of a particular man and painting out all those features which are not essential to men as such. But if we actually did this, the result would be not a picture of man in the abstract, but an empty canvas. By the time we had painted out, say, everything which showed the man to be black or white, fat or thin, bald or hairy, seated or standing, etc., there would be nothing left at all. The analogy between ideas and pictures thus fails to provide us with an intelligible account of abstraction. And although Locke was aware of this, he never went on to provide a satisfactory alternative account.

[4] *Essay Concerning Human Understanding,* "Of Maxims," 9.

It is true that Locke is less wholehearted in his commitment to the theory of ideas as pictures than Berkeley and Hume after him. But he does not offer us any positive alternative theory, and probably could not have done so. The picture theory of ideas is too closely tied up with other aspects of the British Empiricist outlook to be dropped without drastic changes elsewhere. Even within the limits of the picture theory of ideas, however, it is possible to give a more cogent account of general ideas than Locke's, as was in fact done by Berkeley and Hume.

Before leaving Locke, we should take note of another aspect of his views on the problem of universals, namely what he has to say about classification. Locke's purpose here is to attack the conception, derived from Aristotle, of an order of nature to which our system of classification ought to conform. According to this view, in the form in which Locke considers it, different kinds of things are distinguished from each other by the possession of different "essences." These essences are not among the observable properties of the things, but it is nevertheless the presence of a common essence which justifies us in saying that things are of the same kind, e.g., men, horses, or oak trees.

The view Locke opposes to this is that we group things together according to their observable similarities. Having made such a grouping, we then proceed to call them by the same name and speak of them as being of the same kind. And even if the things so grouped should happen to be alike in some respect which is not observable, and which is the cause of the observed similarities, it is not *because* of this that we group them together. Nor is the existence of such a hidden similarity required to justify our grouping.

Locke argues that the view he is attacking is refuted by the existence of "monsters"—deformed or aberrant members of a species. If there is an essence of *man*, whose presence in any object is what makes that object a man, how can such an object fail to exhibit all the distinctive features of man (e.g., by lacking arms or legs)? But we could hardly say that the essence is not present in such a case, for the object is certainly not an animal of any other species.

Berkeley

Berkeley's discussion of general ideas begins with an attack on Locke's doctrine of abstraction. Berkeley rejects completely Locke's view that general ideas, considered simply as ideas, must be of a different character from ideas of particulars. What makes an idea general, for Berkeley, is simply the use we make of it in thought.

As I have already said, Berkeley unlike Locke, is unequivocally committed to the conception of ideas as mental pictures. (In other parts of his work he also speaks of "notions," which are not to be conceived as mental pictures. But the word "idea," at any rate, always means for Berkeley a mental picture.) And his account of general ideas may be seen as an attempt to produce a theory better in line with this conception of ideas than Locke's. But even if we reject the whole apparatus of ideas as conceived by the British Empiricists, as most contemporary philosophers do, Berkeley's account still has the merit of clearly recognizing, as Locke's does not, that one can think in general terms about triangles, for example, without needing to be able to conceive of a triangle which has no properties except its triangularity.

Berkeley's argument against Locke's "abstract general ideas" is based on the premise that one cannot conceive as separated those things which could not possibly exist as separated. Thus it is impossible that there should be motion without there being something which moves, and so, Berkeley argues, we cannot *conceive* motion without something which moves either. Likewise, it is impossible that a man should exist without having some particular color and stature, and therefore it is impossible for us to conceive of a man having no particular color or stature.

Berkeley has often been criticized for identifying the conceivable with the imaginable (i.e., what one can form a mental picture of). But we should note that his point here does not depend on this identification. Motion without something which moves, or a man who has no particular color or stature, are precisely the kinds of things which contemporary philosophers, too, would speak of as "inconceivable." And if Locke's account of abstraction requires us to be able to conceive such things—and as we have seen in the passage about the idea of a triangle, Locke himself is inclined to think that it does—this is a valid argument against it.

Indeed, it may be argued that Berkeley adds nothing to his case by identifying conceiving with imagining, and imagining with the having of a mental image. Arguing for the proposition that one cannot conceive of a man who has no particular color or stature, he says the following: ". . . The idea of man which I frame to myself, must be either of a white, or a black, or a tawny, a straight, or a crooked, a tall, or a low, or a middle-sized man."[5]

If we take this as meaning simply that it is impossible to conceive that a man should have no particular color, or should be of no particular stature, etc., it is undoubtedly true. But if Berkeley is also saying that I

[5] *Principles of Human Knowledge*, Introduction.

cannot imagine a man without imagining him as of some particular color or height, this is false. At least, it is certainly false if "imagining" is taken in its ordinary sense rather than in the much narrower sense of having a mental image. Walking along a dark street, I may imagine that a man is following me, without specifically imagining him as black or white, tall or short, or anything else of the kind. And to imagine this is by no means the same as imagining that a man without any particular color or stature is following me, which may well be impossible.

And even if we identify imagining with having a mental image, it is not clear that the mental image would have to specify the individual features of the man in the way Berkeley supposes. After all, not even an ordinary picture need give any definite indication of a man's height, or of many other things about him. It is true that no picture, mental or otherwise, could count as a picture of a man having no particular height (at least, not in terms of straightforward literal representation, which is what is relevant here). But this is so merely because nothing would count as a man of no particular height, and hence the notion of accurate representation of such a man has no sense.

I think, therefore, that the real force in Berkeley's attack on Locke lies in his assertion that Locke confuses the abstractions, e.g., thinking about a triangle without thinking about the size of its angles, with thinking about a triangle as if its angles *had* no size. We must now look at Berkeley's own alternative account of such matters.

Berkeley's view is that when we think about triangles in general, as opposed to thinking about a particular triangle, the only ideas we need to make use of are ideas of particular triangles.

The generality of our thinking comes out in the use

we make of such ideas. If we refrain from taking into account in our reasoning any of the properties of the triangle we imagine other than its being triangular, then our reasoning will apply to *all* triangles, irrespective of whether they share the peculiarities of the particular triangle we imagine. Hence even if the idea we use is that of an equilateral triangle, its function in our thinking is not to represent equilateral triangles, but simply to represent triangles. It is therefore playing the role of a general idea of triangle, and this, Berkeley holds, is the only sense in which general ideas are possible.

This account was obviously suggested to Berkeley by the procedure followed in geometry, where a diagram is used to facilitate the working out of a proof. Such a diagram will normally contain more information than is relevant to the proof, e.g., the triangle we draw to prove a general theorem about triangles will have its angles of a certain size and its sides of a certain length. But in carrying out the proof, we take care to disregard such irrelevant features of the diagram. Thus, although the same diagram might have served to represent some specific kind of triangle, its actual function is to represent *any* triangle.

Berkeley also recognizes that, just as we sometimes carry out geometrical proofs without using any diagrams at all, we sometimes think in general terms about triangles or men without needing to summon up an idea of a triangle or an idea of a man to do it. However, Berkeley does not by any means infer from this that ideas in his sense could be dispensed with altogether. On the contrary, he regards purely verbal thinking as deriving its meaning from the fact that the ideas corresponding to the words *can* be produced, somewhat as algebra derives its meaning from the fact that the variables *can* be replaced by numbers. A person who is thoroughly familiar with the meaning of "triangle" may use this word in his thoughts without accompanying it by any ideas of triangles, without this in any way impairing his reasonings. But the real test of his understanding of the term is whether he can summon up the appropriate idea (or rather, since many different ideas would, on Berkeley's theory, serve, *an* appropriate idea). Purely verbal thinking is, in Berkeley's opinion, a hazardous activity. There is always the danger that once we have lost sight of the ideas, we may fall into using words in such a way that they do not correspond to ideas at all, and when this happens, as Berkeley thinks it quite often does, our thoughts become empty and meaningless.

Hume

Hume follows Berkeley in rejecting Locke's abstract ideas. Like Berkeley, he holds that general ideas are possible only in the sense that a particular idea may be used, after the manner described above, to represent *any* individual of a given kind. His further development of Berkeley's views mainly concerns the psychological processes involved in this use of ideas.

According to Hume, the processes involved are as follows: "When we have found a resemblance among several objects, that often occur to us, we apply the same name to all of them, whatever differences we may observe in the degrees of their quantity and quality, and whatever other differences may appear among them. After wè have acquired a custom of this kind, the hearing of that name revives the idea of one of these objects, and makes the imagination conceive it with all its particular circumstances and proportions. But as the same word is supposed to have been frequently applied to other individuals, that are different in many respects from that idea, which is immediately present to the mind, the word not being able to revive the idea of all these individuals, only touches the soul, if I may be allowed so to speak, and revives that custom, which we have acquired by surveying them. They are not really and in fact present to the mind, but only in power; nor do we draw them all out distinctly in the imagination, but keep ourselves in a readiness to survey any of them, as we may be prompted by a present design or necessity."[6]

Thus when we hear and understand a general term (or, one may add, when we use such a term with understanding, whether in speaking, writing, or thinking), what happens, according to Hume, is that there comes into our minds the idea of a particular thing of that kind, and at the same time we put ourselves in a state of readiness to produce other ideas of things of that kind as may be required.

What is really new here is the notion of a *state of readiness*. The view that knowing the meaning of a general term involves the capacity to form, not one abstract idea, as in Locke, but any one of a whole range of particular ideas, was already implicit in Berkeley. And Hume of course follows Berkeley in holding that when we use a general term, the idea which comes before our minds will be the idea of a particular thing of the relevant kind. But in addition to the mere capacity which is knowing what the word means, and the overt exercise of this capacity (the forming of an appropriate particular idea), Hume postulates a state of readiness to exercise this capacity in *any* way which may be required. This state of readiness is not to be identified with the capacity itself, nor is it in any

[6] *Treatise of Human Nature,* Introduction.

straightforward sense an exercise of the capacity. Rather, it is a temporary activation of it.

An analogy may help to make Hume's point clear. A person who has learned French and has not forgotten it has the *capacity* to speak French at all times, whether he is actually doing so or not. And when he says something in French, he is *exercising* this capacity. But suppose that he goes to pick up the telephone in the expectation that the person on the line will speak to him in French. Then he is not, as yet, exercising his capacity to speak French, but he is in a state of *readiness* to exercise it, as he was perhaps not a moment before.

We may agree with Hume that some such concept of "readiness" is required for an adequate account of what goes on when someone hears or uses a word with understanding. The weak point in his account is the way in which he interprets this "readiness" as simply the readiness to produce a range of mental images. According to Hume's account, a person who was deficient in mental imagery, and so could not produce mental images of men, could not know what the word "man" meant, and so could not hear or use it with understanding. And this must surely be wrong. We can judge well enough whether a person understands a word without investigating his powers of mental imagery.

Consideration of the British Empiricist Approach

There are two main questions to be raised about the British Empiricist approach to the problem of universals. First, all three philosophers maintain that everything which exists is particular. But we may wonder whether the theories they propound are really consistent with this position. For one thing, they are inclined to speak about ideas and words in a way which implies that ideas and words are *not* particulars. They speak of having the same idea on two different occasions, or using the same word on two different occasions. Ideas and words, so conceived, are entities which have instances, and so are not particulars—though it must be added that they are not universals in the ordinary sense either, for they are not properties of anything.[7] However, it may be that this apparent inconsistency could be overcome by speaking, instead, of classes of similar ideas or classes of similar words. A more serious difficulty is the use made of the concept of similarity. Is it consistent to at the same time maintain that only particulars exist, and that, in Locke's words, "nature, in the production of things, makes several of them alike"? Or does this admission of real similarities—which all three philosophers make—amount to a tacit admission of universals?

This problem will be left for discussion in the next chapter, where we shall be considering the criticisms which later philosophers have brought against the attempt to avoid postulating universals by speaking of similarities between particulars instead. In what remains of this chapter, I want to discuss the second important question, namely, whether the British Empiricist apparatus of "ideas" provides an adequate framework for explaining the functioning of general terms, or indeed of words as such.

We have seen that the only clear account offered of what "ideas" are is that they are mental images. (This is not strictly accurate, since in the terminology of Locke and Berkeley ideas also include what is immedi-

[7] Words conceived of as having instances are in current philosophical usage called "types," and the sounds or inscriptions which constitute their instances are called "tokens." Thus the parenthesis (white, white) would be said to contain two *tokens* of the *type* "white."

ately before the mind in sense perception, i.e., what later philosophers have called "sense data." But it is ideas in the sense of mental images which are mainly in question in the discussions of general terms.) And the most obvious objection to the British Empiricists' approach to the problem of general terms is that it tends to give to mental imagery an importance for thought and for the use of language which it simply does not have.

Thus for both Berkeley and Hume, our ability to use words meaningfully depends on our ability to summon up appropriate mental images—even if we do not actually do so on every occasion. A general term has meaning primarily by being associated with a range of mental images of particular things falling under the term. And as I have already suggested in discussing Hume, we do not in fact need to investigate a person's powers of mental imagery in order to judge whether he has a correct understanding of a given word. Why, then, were Berkeley and Hume led to say things from which it seems to follow that we do?

Part of the explanation lies in a certain confusion surrounding the use of the term "idea." In Berkeley and Hume certainly, and sometimes in Locke as well, it is made clear that we are supposed to think of ideas as mental pictures or images. But at the same time, "having the idea of something" is required to do duty for "thinking of something" or "having something before one's mind." And the result of this is that thinking of something is identified with having a mental image of it.

Once this identification is made, the Berkeley-Hume account of understanding the meaning of a word follows very easily. To hear or use a word with understanding is to hear or use it *thinking of what the word stands for*, or, to adopt Hume's modification, at least in the *readiness* to think of what the word stands for. So to hear or use a word with understanding is to hear or use it in the readiness to form a mental image of what it stands for, or, in the case of a general term, mental images of things of the kind it stands for.

The real objection to this is not that thinking of something is one thing and having a mental image of it another. Rather, it is that there is no such mental act as "thinking of something" at all, if this is supposed to be an act of simply holding the thing before one's mind without thinking anything *about* it. And that is just the kind of act which it is required to be. According to the philosophers we are considering, "thinking of" something, entertaining the idea of it, is an act simpler and more basic than the act of thinking a thought *about* the thing. When we think that snow is white, for example, it is supposed that we have the idea of snow, have also the idea of white, and somehow combine these two ideas into the thought that snow is white. (*How* we do this is, for such a view, a serious problem.) The acts of "thinking of snow" and "thinking of white" are the elements out of which the act of thinking that snow is white is made.

The model for "thinking of something," or "having it before one's mind," is obviously ordinary vision. "Having a thing before one's mind" is to be like having it before one's eyes, except that the object is not actually there. And the nearest thing to seeing an object which can be done in the object's absence is having a mental image of it. But there is a crucial difference between these two things. If I see Jones, it is Jones who is in front of me whether I think it is or not. When I have a mental image of Jones, on the other hand, my image is an image *of Jones* only because, roughly, I *mean* it as an image of Jones. It might be that my image in fact resembles Brown, whom I have never met, rather more than it resembles Jones, but that does not make it an image of Brown rather than of Jones. So the act of having a mental image of Jones necessarily has a complexity which the act of seeing Jones does not have.

This points to a difficulty in the notion of an "idea of a particular" to which I have not so far drawn attention. Berkeley and Hume insist that all ideas, in themselves, are ideas of particulars, it is only by being used in a special way that they become general ideas. But the phrase "idea of a particular" is, as they use it, ambiguous. It may mean "idea such that there is a particular of which it is the idea," as in "idea of Jones," or it may mean merely "idea of a *possible* particular" (as opposed to Locke's abstract ideas, which are not ideas of any possible particulars). I may—or let us agree for argument's sake that I may—have an image which represents a man of a definite color, stature, and all the rest of it, and yet this image may not be meant as the image of any existing man. It is the image of a possible particular, but not of an actual one. So there is at any rate a serious omission in the account given by Berkeley and Hume; they offer an explanation of how the idea of a possible particular comes to represent a *kind of thing*, but they do not explain how the idea of a possible particular comes to represent an *actual* particular.

Indeed, we may even turn Berkeley's problem on its head and ask, not "How is it possible for the idea of a particular to come to represent a kind of thing?", but "How is it possible for the idea of a possible *kind* of particular to come to represent an actual particular?" For it may at least plausibly be held that all that is required to make an image the image of a possible particular is that *there could be a particular which looked like that*. But if there could be one, there could equally well be more than one. So if an image of this kind is to be given an external reference on grounds of resemblance alone, it will have to stand not for one actual particular, but rather for *any object which looks like that*. To make it stand for an actual particular, something more is required, and this something more cannot be anything in the intrinsic nature of the image.

We can see now why the notion of having a mental image of an actual particular as a simple confrontation between the mind and the object is untenable. If we merely have an image of a possible particular, and there is nothing more to it than that, no connection has been made with an object that actually exists. And if such a connection is made, the making of it is something over and above the mere having of the image. It is only in the second case that we might say we were "thinking of" an actual object. This "thinking of," if we call it that, is not something more basic and elementary than thinking complete thoughts, but on the contrary depends on our ability to think complete thoughts (e.g., perhaps, the thought "This is what Jones looks like"). So even mental imagery, which seemed the most likely candidate for the role of "thinking of" something in the sense of a simple confrontation between mind and object, is not in fact fitted to play such a role.

The above considerations also show the question posed by Berkeley and Hume, "How do particular ideas become general?", in a different light. There is no problem of the sort these philosophers have in mind in the notion of a completely determinate image of, say, a particular type of postage stamp serving to represent *any* postage stamp of that type. The problem comes when we consider terms such as "man" or "triangle," for here, whatever image we take, we cannot explain the meaning of "man" or "triangle" simply by saying "A man (or a triangle) is something which looks like *this*." So there has to be a range of images instead.

What are we now to make of the suggestion that to hear or use a word with understanding is to hear or use it either thinking of what the word stands for, or at least in the readiness to think of what it stands for? The interpretation of this in terms of images has now shown itself to be ambiguous. When I hear the word "man," is it enough that I should respond with images of *possible* men, or ought I to respond with images of men that actually exist?

Being unaware of the ambiguity, Berkeley and Hume did not ask themselves this question. But in view of the account they give of abstract thinking, it is clear that at least *sometimes* images of possible men would be enough. Consider the following passage from Hume: ". . . One of the most extraordinary circumstances in the present affair, [is] that after the mind has produced an individual idea, upon which we reason, the attendant custom, revived by the general or abstract term, readily suggests any other individual, if by chance we form any reasoning that agrees not with it."[8]

In the example Hume uses, where someone, using the idea of an equilateral triangle, thinks "the angles of a triangle are equal," and then rapidly calls to mind images of other kinds of triangle, it is clear that the image of a possible particular is sufficient. All we need to be reminded of is that a figure which looks like *that* is also a triangle, and its angles are not equal.

But in other cases this is plainly not so. Suppose someone says "All red-headed people are temperamental." It would hardly be to the purpose for me to call up the image of an imaginary red-headed person wearing a placid expression. But if the image was intended as the image of Mary, a red-headed acquaintance whom I know to be characteristically placid, then what Hume

[8] *Treatise of Human Nature*, Introduction.

has in mind would occur. I would become aware that the generalization was false. So if we are trying to save Hume's theory, we shall have to insist that sometimes we must be ready to call up not merely the image of a possible thing of the relevant kind, but the image of an *actual* thing of the relevant kind.

However, it must be becoming obvious by now that the theory cannot be saved, at least not insofar as it relies on images. In the above example, it is clear that my image of Mary plays no essential role. It would serve the purpose just as well if I merely said to myself "No, that's not true, because Mary has red hair and she is placid," without calling up any images at all. And this, generalized, is surely the only tenable interpretation of Hume's theory; namely, that to hear or use a word with understanding is to do so in the readiness to call to mind *any relevant information one has about things of that kind*, and whether we produce any imagery in the process is immaterial. It is the readiness to do this which makes the difference between understanding and merely hearing the words, as for instance if someone says "Of course, man is extinct," and I hear his words but simply nod.

Even if it is granted that we can explain the notion of hearing or using a word with understanding without reference to imagery, however, it may still be asked whether we can explain *knowing the meaning of a word* without reference to imagery. But surely we can. If imagery is not required in the day-to-day use of words, the only other possibility is that it is required in the process of *learning* to use them. And it is of course true that we cannot know what the word "man" means until we know what men are like. But this does not require the use of imagery—we can, and in fact do, learn what men are like by observing actual men, rather than by having images of men. It seems, therefore, that the task of explaining the function of general terms, or of words as such, can and should be carried out without reference to imagery.

It may finally be asked whether, even if we do not need images, we may still need "ideas" in some sense such as that contemplated by the British Empiricists, only without identifying them with images. The answer to this depends on the view we take of the notion of "thinking of" something, in the sense considered above. If we reject this notion, there is no room for "ideas," for the function of "ideas" is to be what is immediately before the mind when we "think of" something, and so if there is no such act, there are no "ideas" in this sense either. I would wish to argue that this is in fact the case, though a full argument cannot be given here.

Chapter Three

RECURRENCE AND RESEMBLANCE

In the previous two chapters, we have considered the theories of universals put forward by various specific philosophers. But the Recurrence and Resemblance theories, which we shall be considering in this chapter, cannot in the same way be labeled with the names of particular philosophers. Rather, they are two possible types of view which in the present century have formed the starting point for discussions of universals in the work of many different philosophers. They represent the attempts of these philosophers to formulate what seemed to them the most plausible versions of realism and of anti-realism, without relating either too closely to specific views on other philosophical questions.

Let us begin by noting the common ground which exists between the two theories. Both the Recurrence Theory and the Resemblance Theory agree that our use of general terms is not merely arbitrary—we apply the same term to many things because something about the things makes this appropriate. And both theories aim at giving a general explanation of what this something is. What they disagree about is the form this explanation should take. Should we explain the non-arbitrariness of general terms by saying that we apply the same general term to things which *share a common property*, or should we explain it by saying that we apply the same general term to things which *resemble* each other?

According to the Recurrence Theory, the application of general terms can be explained only by reference to common properties and relations. We call both A and B "red" because the same property of *redness* occurs in both of them; we say both that A is larger than B and that C is larger than D because the same relation of *being larger than* holds between each of the two pairs. There are thus genuinely recurring properties and relations, in the sense that one and the same property may belong to two different objects, and one and the same relation may hold between two different pairs of objects.

According to the Resemblance Theory, we ought to dispense with common properties and relations and explain the application of general terms as based on resemblance. We call both A and B "red" because they resemble each other in a certain way. And likewise, we say both that A is larger than B and that C is larger than D because the two pairs A and B, C and D, are similarly related. The resemblance on which the application of a general term is based is sometimes explained as resemblance to a "standard particular." Thus, it is suggested, we might explain the term "red" as applying to all things which resemble some red object chosen as a standard, such as a sample in a color chart.

Thus the Recurrence Theory asserts the existence of genuinely recurring common properties and relations, while the Resemblance Theory maintains that there are only individual things which resemble and differ from each other in various ways.

I shall now consider some of the main arguments which have been put forward in the debate over the respective merits of the two theories.

The first argument (put forward by R. I. Aaron)[1] purports to derive the existence of common qualities from the existence of things which *exactly resemble* each other. By "things which exactly resemble each other" is meant things which are exactly the same color, or exactly the same shape, or exactly the same weight, etc., or which have the sort of over-all exact resemblance which may exist between, say, two postage stamps or two ping-pong balls.

In cases such as these, it is argued, it is surely impossible to deny the existence of a common property. If two things are *exactly* the same color, how can we possibly deny that one and the same color is to be found in both of them?

Before attempting to criticize this argument, we should note that it does not claim to prove that *all* general terms are to be explained as corresponding to common properties or relations. It concerns only those terms for which there is an *exact* resemblance between all things falling under the term (what I shall call here "exact-resemblance terms"), and plainly not all terms are of this kind. For example, all red things are *not* exactly the same color. So at best the argument provides only partial support for the Recurrence Theory.

An exact-resemblance term may be defined as a term such that if it applies to A, then it will also apply to B if and only if B is in a certain respect exactly similar to A. Aaron offers as examples of such terms the names of precise shades of color, such as "ultramarine" or "royal blue." Of course, these terms may not always or indeed often be used as exact-resemblance terms: we could in many contexts distinguish between different shades of ultramarine or different shades of royal blue. But one can also imagine their being used as

[1] Aaron, R. I., *The Theory of Universals* (New York and London, 1967), "Common Qualities."

exact-resemblance terms, perhaps in connection with a color chart. ("To be ultramarine, it must be *exactly* like the sample in the chart.") In the following discussion, I shall assume that they are being used in this way, and by contrast I shall use "blue" as an example of a color-word which is not an exact-resemblance term.

Aaron clearly thinks that there are reasons for accepting the inference "A and B are both ultramarine, therefore there is a property which A and B share" which are not available in the case of the inference "A and B are both blue, therefore etc." And his point is apparently this. Opposing the second inference, the Resemblance Theorist may say "Blue things don't share a common color, they are merely similar." But he cannot oppose the first inference by saying "Ultramarine things don't share a common color, they are merely similar." For how can he pretend that ultramarine things are *merely* similar?

But this argument seems to be exploiting an ambiguity in the phrase "merely similar." "Merely similar" is sometimes used in contrast to "exactly similar." In this sense, ultramarine things are certainly not merely similar. However, the Resemblance Theorist need not deny this. For he could be using "merely similar" not in contrast to "exactly similar," but only in contrast to "having a common property" or "sharing the same color." So he can consistently say "Ultramarine things are similar, indeed, *exactly* similar, but they don't share a common color. It is *merely a question of similarity*, and none the less so because the similarity happens to be an exact one."

Or can he? Suppose we argue on Aaron's side as follows. Let A be an ultramarine thing and B another ultramarine thing. Then A and B must be exactly similar in color. Hence the color of A is identical with the color of B. And to grant this is to grant the existence of a genuinely recurring property.

The plausibility of this argument comes from the fact that in ordinary usage there seems to be no significant difference between saying that A is exactly the same color as B and saying that the color of A is identical with the color of B. But the Resemblance Theorist may defend his position as follows: "When you say that the color of A is identical with the color of B, I accept this if it is nothing but another way of saying that A and B are exactly the same color. But if you mean anything *more*, namely that there really is an entity called 'the color of A' which is identical with an entity called 'the color of B,' then I deny this. And if you *don't* mean anything more, you are really only arguing that if things are exactly the same color, they are exactly the same color, which is trivial."

This is one possible line of defense. However, some supporters of the Recurrence Theory have instead taken the line of arguing that no two things *are* ever exactly similar, in color or in any other respect, on the ground that we can never be sure that there is not a difference which we are unable to detect.[2]

Let us now consider a closely related argument against the Recurrence Theory. Aaron, as we have seen,

[2] The notion of "exact resemblance" indeed raises problems of its own. Colors, for example, are called "exactly similar" if they are *indistinguishable*, i.e., we cannot see any difference between them. But suppose, as may well happen, that *you* can see a difference and I can't? Or suppose there is a difference which no human being can detect, but which seems to be perceptible to some other species? Should "exact resemblance" be defined relative to all possible perceivers ("no human being, and indeed no creature, will ever detect a difference"), or relative to a given perceiver ("they are exactly similar *to me*, since *I* can't detect a difference"). Either course presents difficulties.

claims that the existence of things which exactly resemble each other establishes the existence of common properties; not, indeed, in the sense of showing that every general term corresponds to a property, but in the sense of showing that every *exact-resemblance* general term corresponds to a property. This conclusion, though not adequate fully to establish the Recurrence Theory, would at least be adequate to refute the Resemblance Theory.

On the other side, it has been argued that the existence of general terms which are *not* exact-resemblance terms refutes the Recurrence Theory, because such terms cannot correspond to properties. For example, all blue things are not exactly alike in color—a sky blue thing is not exactly the same color as an ultramarine thing. If this is so, it is argued, the color of the one cannot be identical with the color of the other, and therefore they do not share a common property.

To this argument the Recurrence Theorist may reply as follows. If by *the* color of an object we mean its exact-resemblance color, i.e., the color possessed by all those things which are exactly similar in color to itself, then certainly *the* color of the sky blue thing is not identical with *the* color of the ultramarine thing. But we may still claim that there is *a* color which is possessed by the sky blue thing, and which is identical with *a* color possessed by the ultramarine thing, namely the color blue. Admittedly blue is not an exact-resemblance color, but for the opponent to assume that all colors must be exact-resemblance colors would be to beg the question.

The Recurrence Theorist may then be asked if the sky blue object has *two* colors, namely blue and sky blue? Of course it is true that it is blue and also that it is sky blue. But are we to say that blue and sky blue are different colors, or that they are one and the same color? They cannot be one and the same, because some things are blue which are not sky blue. But it seems no more satisfactory to say that they are different.

However, this is not a difficulty peculiar to discussion of properties. It arises equally if we ask "Is my arm the same physical object as my whole body, or a different physical object?" If this is not an objection to assuming the existence of physical objects, the Recurrence Theorist may argue, it is not an objection to assuming the existence of properties either.

A second argument which has been advanced against the Recurrence Theory concerns the existence of general terms which are to some extent vague in their meaning and therefore admit of borderline cases. For example, some objects are definitely white, others are definitely not white, and others again may be regarded as marginal cases, lying within the area in which white shades off into, say, pale gray or cream. And the existence of such marginal cases seems to pose a problem for the Recurrence Theory. In ordinary speech we may dispose of them by calling the object "whitish" or "nearly white." But in the language of the Recurrence Theory we have to say either that the object *has* the property of whiteness, or that it has *not*. And there seems to be no room for any intermediate possibility.

To this it may be replied that the language of the Recurrence Theory is not really any more misleading in this respect than everyday language. For although in everyday language we have ways of indicating that an object is a marginal case for the application of the term "white," we still have the problem of what to say about the statement "This is white" itself. The assumption that this statement is either true or false is no easier to reconcile with the existence of marginal cases than the assumption that a thing either has, or does not have, the property of whiteness. The difficulty the Recurrence Theory is faced with thus merely duplicates a difficulty which we are already faced with in everyday speech.

But on behalf of the Resemblance Theory it may be claimed that a philosophical theory ought to be able to account for such difficulties instead of merely duplicating them, and that the Resemblance Theory, unlike its rival, is able to do this. For according to the Resemblance Theory, the term "white" applies to each of a class of things which resemble each other. Of these, some will be indisputable examples of whiteness, while others will resemble these central cases more or less closely. And since resemblance is obviously a matter of degree, it is entirely in keeping with the theory that these should be marginal cases, where the resemblance to the central cases is enough to tempt us to apply the term "white," but not close enough for us to classify the thing as white without qualification. Thus if we follow the Resemblance Theory, marginal cases become something to be expected rather than constituting a difficulty.

A possible counterargument here is for the Resemblance Theorist to offer his own method of dealing with the difficulty, by maintaining that vague words do not in any straightforward sense correspond to properties. As long as the term "white" is used with the vagueness it has in most everyday speech, we cannot speak of a property of whiteness as such. Rather, we should associate the term "white" with a certain *range* of properties, corresponding to the various ways in which its meaning could be made more precise. In ordinary speech, it is simply left indeterminate which of these properties the term "white" stands for.

We must now consider the best-known argument against the Resemblance Theory, that advanced by Bertrand Russell. Russell argues that the Resemblance

Theory cannot avoid recognizing resemblance itself as a genuine universal, and can therefore at most succeed in reducing the number of universals to one. And if one universal at least has to be admitted, he suggests, there is little point in refusing to admit other universals as well.[8]

The version of Russell's argument I shall consider is taken from his early book *Problems of Philosophy*. In his later work he varied the formulation of the argument slightly, but without substantially changing it. The *Problems of Philosophy* version is as follows: "If we wish to avoid the universals *whiteness* and *triangularity*, we shall choose some particular patch of white or some particular triangle, and say that anything is white or a triangle if it has the right sort of resemblance to our chosen particular. But then the resemblance required will have to be a universal. Since there are many white things, the resemblance will have to hold between many pairs of particular white things; and this is the characteristic of a universal. It will be useless to say that there is a different resemblance for each pair, for then we shall have to say that these resemblances resemble each other, and thus at last we shall be forced to admit resemblance as a universal. The relation of resemblance, therefore, must be a true universal."

Russell's first point here is a very simple one. He presents the Resemblance Theorist as saying "There are no universals, there are only resemblances," and to this he replies that resemblances (being relations of a certain kind) are themselves universals. So by conceding that resemblances exist, the Resemblance Theorist has in fact conceded that universals exist.

The Resemblance Theorist can evade this conclu-

[8] Küng (Küng, G., *Ontology and the Logistic Analysis of Language* [New York, 1968], Chapter 5) points out that this argument was anticipated by Husserl, and before him by Mill.

sion only by denying that he really is conceding the existence of resemblances in the sense supposed. Russell presents him as denying that the resemblances whose existence he asserts are universals at all. It seems to be possible to speak of the *resemblance between* A *and* B as a particular, something which by definition cannot hold between any other two things (as we might also speak of *the redness of this carpet* as a particular belonging to this carpet alone, perhaps in much the same way that the surface of this carpet belongs to this carpet alone). The Resemblance Theorist can thus argue that the only resemblances whose existence is required by his theory are *particular resemblances* in this special sense.

But there is another line which he might take instead. He might say "I am not actually suggesting that *resemblances exist* at all, though I may sometimes carelessly speak as though I were. What I am saying is only that *things exist and sometimes they resemble each other.*"

Russell's reply to the first line of defense is as follows. Suppose the Resemblance Theorist has said "White things are those things which have a certain resemblance R to the standard white particular W." It is then pointed out that the resemblance R is itself a universal. So the Resemblance Theorist says "Actually I don't really mean that there is such a resemblance R. When I say that the various white things W_1, W_2, etc., all have a resemblance R to the standard particular W, what I mean is that W_1 has a certain particular resemblance R_1 to W, W_2 has another particular resemblance R_2 to W, and so on."

But these particular resemblances R_1, R_2, etc. must be somehow alike. For they are all supposed to be resemblances in respect of color (and not, for example, resemblances in respect of shape). So the Resemblance

Theorist is obliged to postulate a new resemblance R_R which holds between the various particular resemblances R_1, R_2, etc. And this too threatens to be a universal. So the Resemblance Theorist must now reduce R_R itself to a class of particular resemblances, which in turn will have to resemble each other, and so on ad infinitum.

Even if the need to distinguish between different kinds of resemblances could be avoided (whether at the stage of R_1, R_2, etc., or at some later stage), this would not solve the problem. For any particular resemblances introduced would still have to resemble each other, even if only in respect of *being resemblances*. It thus seems that the program of eliminating resemblances which are universals in favor of resemblances which are particulars can never be completed.

But what about the second line of defense? Suppose the Resemblance Theorist says "I didn't really mean that the white things all *have a certain resemblance* to the standard particular W. All I meant is that they *resemble* it, and in saying this I am not implying the existence of any entity called a 'resemblance.'"

There are two points to be considered here. First, the Resemblance Theorist now wants to distinguish between asserting the existence of entities called "resemblances" and merely asserting that things sometimes resemble each other, and claims that he can do the latter while refraining from doing the former. This claim may be challenged. And secondly, even if the claim is accepted in principle, it may be argued that the Resemblance Theorist cannot in fact achieve his particular purpose merely by asserting that things sometimes resemble each other.

One obvious way in which the Resemblance Theorist may become vulnerable to the second objection is by speaking of resemblances as themselves resembling each other. When he says "The resemblance between A and B resembles the resemblance between C and D," he certainly seems to be treating resemblances as entities. And he seems to be driven into such ways of speaking by his need to distinguish between different kinds of resemblance. For without so distinguishing, he cannot single out those things which resemble the chosen particular in the relevant respect rather than in some other respect. If, say, the particular chosen to exemplify "white" is square as well as white, he must make clear that the term "white" applies to things which resemble it in color, and not (except by accident) to things which resemble it in shape.

However, the Resemblance Theorist may reply that he can make the required distinctions simply by using a variety of relational terms in place of the one term "resembles." The statement "A is the same color as B" could perhaps be understood as merely saying how the particulars A and B are related to each other, without implying the existence either of entities called "resemblances," or of entities called "colors." To emphasize the intended absence of such implications, we might instead say "A and B are like-colored."

But there are further difficulties. Likeness in color is a matter of degree; a gray thing will be *more* like the chosen white particular W in color than a black thing will. But it will not be like enough to count as white. So we must not only make clear that likeness in color, rather than some other kind of likeness, is relevant, but also specify the *degree* of likeness in color required. This could perhaps be done by a suitable elaboration of the theory, e.g., adding extra chosen particulars to serve as examples of things which are *just* too grayish, too pinkish, etc. to count as white, and then saying "A white thing is one which is *more* like W in color than these are."

Unfortunately such a procedure, though it might work in certain simple cases such as that of colors, cannot easily be generalized. Consider the word "machine." It is hard to see on what principle we could select examples of things which were *not quite* similar enough to some standard example of a machine to count as machines. Such cases at any rate show that the Resemblance Theory, even modified as suggested above, could not be turned into an adequate account of *all* general terms without introducing a great many complications.

Let us turn now to the other objection. Can the Resemblance Theorist legitimately make a distinction between saying that things resemble each other and saying that there are entities called "resemblances"?

It might be held that by using *any* general term we are committing ourselves to the existence of a corresponding entity: if we say "A is white," we are committed to the existence of *whiteness*; if we say "A resembles B," we are committed to the existence of *resemblance*; and so on. But this is not the view taken by Russell. According to Russell, the Resemblance Theorist is able successfully to avoid admitting the existence of the universal *white*, but not, ultimately, that of the universal *resemblance*.

The difference, for Russell, seems to be that the Resemblance Theorist can eliminate the term "white" from his language, for instead of speaking of "white things," he can speak of "things resembling W." But he cannot eliminate the term "resembles" from his language in the same way. Russell thus seems to be assuming that the use of a general term does commit one to admitting a corresponding universal, *unless the general term can be eliminated*. If this interpretation is correct, Russell's argument turns out to be a variant of the argument according to which a term can have meaning only by corresponding to an entity. Only Russell, instead of asserting this of *all* terms, asserts it only of those terms which cannot be eliminated from the language.

Aaron also argues that the Resemblance Theorist is committed to admitting resemblance as a universal. For him, the crucial point is that the Resemblance Theorist regards it as a "fact of nature" that certain things resemble each other. We do not create such resemblances, but discover them. And to say this, according to Aaron, is to concede that such a resemblance is a "universal in nature."[4]

But the Resemblance Theorist may deny that he is conceding this. To say that it is a discoverable *fact* that certain things resemble each other, he may argue, is not to concede the existence of an entity called "resemblance" (which, if it existed, would admittedly be a universal). One may at the same time maintain that particular things really do resemble each other, and insist that the only entities which exist are particulars.

On this view, then, admitting "resemblance" *as an entity* involves something more than admitting it to be a fact that things sometimes resemble each other. And likewise, to admit "redness" *as an entity* involves something more than admitting it to be a fact that some things are red. An attempt to explain what this "something more" might be has been made by W. V. Quine (see below, Chapter 5).

A philosopher taking Aaron's view might retort that even if a legitimate distinction can be made between admitting that things really resemble each other and admitting resemblance as an entity, it is not *this* distinction which is important. What matters is whether we regard ourselves, in our use of general words, as

[4] Aaron, R. I., *The Theory of Universals*, p. 235.

grouping things arbitrarily, or as recognizing groupings which already exist. That our use of general terms is *not* arbitrary is the essential point of realism. And realism in this sense is presupposed by both the Resemblance Theory and the Recurrence Theory, since it is this very non-arbitrariness of general terms which the two theories set out to explain.

We thus have in the problem of universals not one central question, but two, namely (1) Are there any such entities as universals? and (2) Is the use of general terms arbitrary? The view that universals are entities and the view that the use of general terms is not arbitrary may both, with historical justification, be called "realist" views. But we cannot from this alone conclude that whoever holds the one must in consistency also hold the other.

Of the two theories considered in this chapter, the Recurrence Theory suggests that a realist answer to question (2) implies a realist answer to question (1), for the theory tries to explain the non-arbitrariness of general terms by reference to such entities as "properties" and "relations." The Resemblance Theory, on the other hand, attempts, by explaining the non-arbitrariness of general terms *without* reference to such entities, to combine a realist answer to question (2) with an anti-realist answer to question (1).

We have looked at some of the difficulties which each theory faces. But we have not yet asked what the alleged "non-arbitrariness" of general terms is, nor in what sense it needs to be "explained." This will be the topic of the next chapter.

Chapter Four

GENERAL TERMS

We have seen in the previous chapter that the Recurrence and Resemblance theories agree in rejecting the view (usually called "extreme nominalism") that in our use of general terms we group things in a completely arbitrary way. We must now try to see what this distinction between "arbitrary" and "non-arbitrary" grouping amounts to.

Suppose I am putting chessmen into a box with two compartments. I may put the pieces into the box "any old way," without caring which pieces go into which compartment. This would be an example of arbitrary grouping. Or I may put all the black pieces into one compartment and all the white pieces into the other. This would be an example of non-arbitrary grouping.

Now suppose that we picture the act of giving meaning to a general term[1] T as a grouping of all things into two compartments, one labeled "T" and one labeled "not T." We may then ask "Is what we are doing here like what I do when I distribute the chessmen between

[1] For the sake of simplicity, I have throughout this chapter ignored relational terms. In the case of relational terms, the classification or "grouping" would have to be not of individual things, but of pairs (or triples, quadruples, etc.) of things. These would further need to be treated as *ordered* pairs, i.e., a distinction would have to be made between the pair x, y and the pair y, x. The need for this is brought out by such relations as *being greater than:* the pair 5, 3 exemplifies this relation, but the pair 3, 5 does not.

the two compartments of the box 'any old way,' or is it like what I do when I put all the black pieces into one compartment and all the white pieces into the other?"

In terms of this analogy, choosing the first alternative would amount to accepting extreme nominalism, and choosing the second alternative to rejecting it. But is the analogy itself acceptable?

The first point to consider is the use made of the idea of "giving meaning to a term." It is not in doubt that people sometimes do something which answers to this description: for example, a scientist or other specialist introducing a new technical term. But this is an act performed by someone who already has a language, and who makes use of this language in explaining what his new term is to mean. And relatively few terms are in fact introduced in this way.

Our analogy, however, invites us to think of *all* general terms as having been given meaning by an act performed by a particular individual on a particular occasion. And it cannot be seriously supposed that all the general terms we have did, in fact, acquire their meanings in this way. So what is in question here is a myth of the origins of language. We are invited to imagine Man, as yet without a language (or at least, without general terms), introducing general terms for the first time, and to choose between two rival descriptions of what he would be doing.

According to both descriptions, his action in introducing a new general term T is comparable to distributing all things between two boxes, one labeled "T" and the other labeled "not T." But the idea of thus distributing *all* things is farfetched even as a myth. So let us modify the image and suppose that he has only the box labeled "T." Then the things he puts into this box will be those to which the term T is to apply, and the things left outside will be those to which it is not to apply.

Once this action of giving a meaning to a term has been completed, the meaning of that term is fixed, and we may henceforward speak of *right* and *wrong* uses of it. Anyone who applies the term T to something which was put in the box labeled "T" will be applying it rightly, and anyone who applies it to anything else will be applying it wrongly. So if subsequent speakers are to be capable of using T correctly, information as to which things were put in the box must somehow be transmitted to them. We may imagine a list of these things being compiled and kept available for reference.

At this point a serious flaw in the myth becomes apparent. It will not do to suppose that knowing the meaning of T is like being in possession of the complete list of Ts—whether by having memorized it or by actually carrying a copy. I know the meaning of the term "cat." But if all the cats in existence had been given names, I would not be capable of listing these names. Nor could I in any other manner draw up an inventory of all currently existing cats. So whatever knowing the meaning of "cat" may be, it is *not* like being in possession of a list.

What, in any case, would the complete list of cats look like? It is supposed to be a list of *all* things to which the term "cat" may correctly be applied. So it cannot be merely a list of the cats existing when the term "cat" was introduced. It must be a list of all cats which ever have existed or ever will exist.

Thus if we imagine someone giving meaning to the term "cat" by putting into one box all the things he intends "cat" to apply to, we must imagine him putting into the box not only all cats existing at the time, but also all cats which have ceased to exist or which have not yet been born. And even as a myth this will hardly do. What has gone wrong?

Suppose C_1, C_2, . . . ,C_n are some cats, and I put them all into a box. Then it follows that I have put C_1 into the box, that I have put C_2 into the box, and so on. But if someone in the distant past had decided to give "cat" the meaning it now has, and Tabitha is a cat, it does *not* follow that he decided to make the term "cat" apply to Tabitha. For neither the physical presence, nor the name, nor even the thought of Tabitha need have played any part in what he did.

The analogy between giving the term "cat" its meaning and putting all cats into a box breaks down because putting all cats into a box (if this were possible, which as we have seen it is not) would be an action in which *each individual cat* was physically involved. But it is not the case that *each individual cat* would have to be physically involved in the action of giving "cat" its meaning. And it will not do, either, to say that the *name* or *idea* of each individual cat would have to be involved.

Thus, to return to our original image, giving meaning to a general term T cannot be like putting the chessmen into the two compartments of their box "any old way," and it cannot be like putting the black pieces in one compartment and the white pieces in the other either. For it is not like distributing all things into two compartments labeled "T" and "not T" at all.

The following seems to be an improvement. In order to give a meaning to T, I put some things in the "T" box and some things in the "not T" box. And I say "I propose that 'T' should be used *in this way*." The difference is that the things in the "T" box are offered only as a *sample* of the things to be called T, and likewise for the things in the "not T" box. Philosophers have called such a procedure "ostensive definition."

In this ostensive definition, only some of the things to be called T are actually involved. But the procedure is nevertheless supposed to determine for *any* particular thing whether or not it is to be called T. How is this possible?

The Recurrence and Resemblance theories may be seen as offering rival answers to this question. Following the Recurrence Theory, I might show you the two boxes and say "Look, *these* things all have a property which none of *those* have. I want you to apply T to whichever things have that property." Or following the Resemblance Theory, I might say "Look, *these* things are like each other and different from *those*. I want you to apply T to whichever things are similarly like these and different from those."

I have also described the Recurrence and Resemblance theories as offering rival explanations of the "non-arbitrariness" of general terms. This suggests that the problem of explaining this "non-arbitrariness" could be identified with the problem of explaining how ostensive definition is possible.

Consider the case of the chessmen. If I put two black pieces in one compartment and two white pieces in the other and tell you to go on in the same way, the chances are you will understand what I want. But if I put several pieces into each compartment "any old way," you may be at a loss to see how to proceed. And we might explain this by saying that you know how to go on in the first case, but don't in the second, because in the first case I am grouping *according to a principle,* whereas in the second case I am grouping *arbitrarily.*

It might accordingly be suggested that ostensive definition can work only when the "ostension," or illustration of the intended meaning of the term, represents a non-arbitrary grouping. To explain how ostensive definition is possible, therefore, we must explain what a non-arbitrary grouping is. According to the Recurrence Theory, it is a grouping on the basis of a common property; according to the Resemblance Theory, it is a grouping on the basis of a resemblance. So it is the existence of common properties (or the fact that things sometimes resemble each other) which makes ostensive definition possible.

And we might go on to argue that it is the possibility of ostensive definition which makes the use of general words possible. For even if actual ostensive *definition*, in the sense of using ostension to introduce a completely new word into the language, never occurred at all, ostensive *learning* (i.e., learning the meaning of a general term from being shown examples) would still have to occur. The only other way of learning the meaning of a general term seems to be from a verbal explanation, and this presupposes some terms learned ostensively as a starting point. And it seems plausible to suppose that ostensive learning is possible only where ostensive definition would have been possible too.

Thus the problem of explaining the conditions under which ostensive definition is possible, the problem of explaining the meaning of non-arbitrary grouping, and the problem of explaining the conditions under which the use of general terms is possible may be seen as three aspects of one and the same problem.

This is a suitable point at which to discuss the claim made by Renford Bambrough in his paper "Universals and Family Resemblances." Bambrough claims (1) that Wittgenstein in his later philosophy succeeds in refuting *both* extreme nominalism *and* realism (of the kind exemplified by the Recurrence and Resemblance theories), and (2) that in so doing, he "solved the problem of universals." It is the first of these claims which I wish to discuss here.

Bambrough takes as his starting point Wittgenstein's introduction of the idea of "family resemblances." Wittgenstein suggests that if we ask what all the things called "games" have in common, we find no one common feature, but rather a "complicated network of similarities, overlapping and criss-crossing: sometimes overall similarities, sometimes similarities of detail." Wittgenstein goes on to say "I can think of no better expression to characterize these similarities than 'family resemblances'; for the various resemblances between the members of a family: build, features, color of eyes, gait, temperament, etc., overlap and criss-cross in the same way. And I shall say: 'games' form a family."[2]

On the face of it, Wittgenstein is suggesting here that there need not be anything in common between the various things to which we apply the same general term. But this is not quite how Bambrough interprets him. Bambrough expresses his view of the relations between extreme nominalism, realism, and the position of Wittgenstein as follows: "The nominalist says that games have nothing in common except that they are called games. The realist says that games must have something in common, and he means by this that they must have something in common other than that they are games. Wittgenstein says that games have nothing in common except that they are games. . . . He asserts at one and the same time the realist's claim that there is an objective justification for the application of the word 'game' to games and the nominalist's claim that there is no element that is common to all games."[3]

It seems at first sight odd to suggest that for a realist,

[2] Wittgenstein, *Philosophical Investigations*, 66.

[3] Bambrough, "Universals and Family Resemblances," *Proceedings of the Aristotelian Society*, LX (1960–61).

games must have something in common other than their being games. But this comment may be explained as follows. A realist view, in the sense in which *both* Recurrence and Resemblance theories are realist views, not only claims that there is an "objective justification" for the application of general terms, but also offers an account of what this justification is. The holder of such a view says "We apply the same general term to things *because* of something about the things." And he would not regard it as a satisfactory account of this "something about the things" to say, for example, that we call things "games" because they are games. Instead he will say that the things all participate in the same Form (Plato), all have the same common property (Recurrence Theory), or all resemble each other in a certain way (Resemblance Theory). Such a statement about the things called 'games' is, according to the realist, explanatory in a way that merely saying they *are* games is not. This, I think, is what Bambrough correctly takes Wittgenstein to have denied.

Why does the realist take this view? Suppose, first, that we have an indefinitely large number of things a, b, c, d, etc., and want to introduce a general term T which will apply to some of these things. As we have seen, we cannot give meaning to T by individually picking out all the things to which T is to apply.

But suppose we imagine the things to be arranged in "chains," e.g., a.....b.....e.....m....., c.....d.....h.....n....., i.....j.... q.....s....., etc. (We may imagine each chain as continuing indefinitely.) T may now be explained as applying to, say, c and everything else in the same chain. In general, things called by the same general term will be things in the same chain. So we can explain how ostensive definition is possible. Once c has been pointed out as something to which T applies, we can decide whether T is to apply to any other thing by finding out whether the other thing is in the same chain as c. Thus we find, for example, that T is to be applied to h, but not to b, although our explanation of the meaning of T made no reference to either h or b.

The problem is to find a suitable interpretation of the connecting relation which we have represented by dotted lines. Obviously it has to be a relation which holds between any two things falling under the same general term. At first sight, therefore, such relations as *participating in the same Form, sharing a common property,* or *having a certain kind of resemblance* appear plausible candidates.

Suppose we have found a suitable connecting relation—let us call it R. Then for any general term T, we can characterize the things to which T applies as those which have R to x, where x is some example of a thing to which T applies. So instead of saying that the term "game" applies to games, we may say, for example, that it applies to things which have R to football, or R to chess. Thus in finding a connecting relation we would also have found the means of completing such sentences as "The term 'game' applies to . . ." or "The term 'red' applies to . . ." without using the words "game" or "red."

Indeed, the connecting relation *has* to be one which can be expressed in this way. For "x Ry" (where "R" expresses the connecting relation) is required to hold if x and y both fall under the term "game," *or* if they both fall under the term "red," *or* if they both fall under any other general term. So the relation R itself cannot be tied to one particular such term. And because of this characteristic of R, we can also make the general claim "Things falling under the same general term always bear the relation R to each other."

One typical kind of account of the connecting relation is that which represents things falling under the same general term as related to each other in virtue of being similarly related to a certain abstract entity. Particulars falling under the same term, according to Plato, participate in *the same Form;* according to the Recurrence Theory, they share *the same property.* The Resemblance Theory, on the other hand, is best seen as an attempt to provide a connecting relation which makes no such reference to an abstract entity. This, indeed, is its main attraction.

The idea of things falling under the same general term, as related to each other in virtue of a common relation to an abstract entity, is no doubt what Bambrough primarily has in mind when he speaks of the realist as holding that games have something in common *other* than their being games. What they "have in common" is the abstract entity which, according to such a view, must be brought in to explain their relation to each other.

The Resemblance Theory differs from such realist theories in that it attempts to avoid the reference to an abstract entity. But it shares with them the aim of seeking for what I have called a connecting relation. And the rejection of this aim is, I would suggest, the essential feature of the view which Bambrough attributes to Wittgenstein. For if Wittgenstein had not rejected it, we would have to regard him as offering a new variant of the Resemblance Theory (based on "family resemblances" instead of resemblances of a less complex kind) and not, as Bambrough claims, as making a radical departure from all previous views.

What objections are there to the idea of a connecting relation? First, we must notice that we have so far ignored the fact that any given thing will fall under *many* general terms. For example, a red apple falls under both the term "red" and the term "apple." So if

R is the connecting relation, the red apple will have R both to a red carpet and to a green apple. Hence it is not possible, as we imagined, to characterize the things called "red" by pointing out one such thing and saying that "red" applies to whatever has R to this thing. For if the thing pointed out were the red apple, it would follow that "red" also applies to the green apple, which of course it does not.

Thus if R is a relation which holds between x and y whenever there is a general term which applies to both x and y (which it must be to perform its role in the type of theory we are considering), it will *not* be the case that if y has R to x and the term T applies to x, then T must also apply to y. So we cannot characterize the things to which T applies as *those which have R to x.*

The position seems more promising if we point out several things, say a red apple, a red tomato, and a red book, and characterize the things to which "red" applies as those which have R to *all* of these things. But this as it stands will not work either. A green apple would have R to all three things, since, like each of them, it falls under the term "solid."

Can this kind of difficulty be overcome by using more examples? In this connection, it is relevant to notice Wittgenstein's discussion in the *Philosophical Investigations* of a rather similar point, that of developing a series of numbers. Wittgenstein suggests that however far we develop a series, we never reach a stage at which there is only one possible way of going on.

Take the series of the numbers in their usual order 1, 2, 3, . . . , etc. Suppose we develop this series up to, say, 3001, and instruct someone to "go on in the same way." In practice, no doubt, he would go on "3002, 3003, . . . , etc." But he *might* have gone on "1, 2, 3, . . . , 3001; 1, 2, 3, . . . , 3001; etc.," or "2, 3, 4, . . . ,

3002; 3, 4, 5, . . . , 3003, etc." And if he did, according to Wittgenstein, we would have no right to object that he is not going on *as we started*, though indeed he is not going on *as we would have gone on*. For if by a "series" we understand a list of numbers generated in accordance with a principle, what he does merits the description "continuing a series" as much as what we would have done.

The analogous point about general terms—and Wittgenstein surely intended such an analogy—would be this. Instead of a list of numbers, consider a list of *things*, intended as an illustration of the meaning of some general term. We show someone this list and, by way of testing his understanding of the term, ask him to add some more things to the list. However long we make the list, he always *might* add something which does not fall under the term we had in mind. And if he does this, we have no right to say he is not following a principle at all, i.e., is not attributing *any* meaning to the term. For he may merely be attributing to it a meaning different from that which we intended.

If this is correct, no list of examples, however long, can fully determine the meaning of the general term the examples are intended to illustrate. We must therefore abandon the hope that if we make the list long enough we can unambiguously fix the meaning of the term by laying down that it applies to whatever has R to all the things on the list.

The point might be supported by the following argument. Suppose we have a list of things a_1, a_2, . . . , a_n. Then one possible term which the list might illustrate would have the meaning "exactly similar to a_1, *or* to a_2, . . . , *or* to a_n." For since, trivially, everything is exactly similar to itself, each of the things a_1, a_2, . . . , a_n would fall under this term. Now let a_{n+1} be some new thing which is not exactly similar to any of a_1,

$a_2, \ldots, a_n$. A second general term could then have the meaning "exactly similar to a_1, *or* to $a_2, \ldots,$ *or* to a_n, *or* to a_{n+1}." This term too would apply to everything on the original list $a_1, a_2, \ldots, a_n$. But since this term applies to a_{n+1} and the previous term does not, they cannot have the same meaning.

It might be suggested that we could account for this kind of ambiguity by postulating not one connecting relation, but many different ones. If the one connecting relation was supposed to be that of "sharing a common property," or "being alike in some respect," the many connecting relations might be of the type "sharing the same color" or "being alike in color," "sharing the same shape" or "being alike in shape," and so forth. We might then argue that a list is by itself ambiguous, because we need to know *which* connecting relation is relevant. But once the relation is specified, the ambiguity disappears.

It is against this suggestion that Wittgenstein's concept of "family resemblances" is most relevant. If Wittgenstein is right in claiming that there is no respect in which all of the things called "games" resemble each other, but only a number of respects in which *some* of them resemble *some* of the others, no suitable connecting relation could be found in this case. We could if we liked say that the things resemble each other *in being games*, but we could not point to any connecting relation which could be understood independently of understanding the meaning of "game" itself. We could show someone what the relation was only by showing him which things we call "games."

I have suggested that Wittgenstein may be seen as differing from both the Recurrence Theory and the Resemblance Theory (among others) in that he rejects the search for a connecting relation, and that this helps to explain Bambrough's contention that Wittgenstein, unlike the realist, maintains that "games have nothing in common except that they are games." But what about the difference which, according to Bambrough, exists between Wittgenstein and the extreme nominalist?

This may be brought out by reverting to the analogy with developing a series. In terms of this analogy, the equivalent of extreme nominalism would be the view that what we call "developing a series" is really no different from what we call "writing down whatever numbers we please." This is surely wrong. But there is a real problem of explaining what the difference is, and this is a problem to which Wittgenstein gives much attention in his discussions of "following a rule."

Suppose that someone is writing down a list of numbers, and at a given moment has written down n numbers. Then we can always discover *some* rule for developing a series, such that the first n numbers in the series would be just those numbers which he has written. But the finding of such a rule does not by itself show that he is developing a series. For the fact that the numbers fit the rule does not establish that he was in any sense *following* the rule.

We may test the hypothesis that he is following the rule by asking him to list more numbers. If these new numbers also fit the rule, we would take this as evidence supporting the correctness of our hypothesis. And if we repeat our request with the same result, we will consider the evidence to be that much stronger.

What happens here may be thought of as follows. *He* writes down numbers, and *we*, independently, write down numbers. And at each stage, we find that the numbers *he* has so far written coincide with those *we* have so far written. Now we have supposed that *we*, at any rate, are making use of an explicitly stated rule. But one can imagine the following situation. A writes down numbers while B watches him. After a while, B says, "Yes, now I see how to go on." B then leaves the room, and both of them write down some more numbers, say twenty more. They are subsequently found to have written the *same* twenty numbers.

In such a situation, we would say that A, without stating an explicit rule, has nevertheless succeeded in teaching B how to develop a certain series. And we could say this even if when challenged, both of them proved incapable of stating the rule according to which they were proceeding.

This imaginary situation is analogous to a perfectly familiar situation involving general words. A child hears its parents calling certain things "red," and eventually it learns to apply the term "red" to (roughly) those things which the parents too would call "red," and to do this *without* needing to hear what the parent says about this or that particular thing. And this, we might argue, provides the best kind of reason we could hope for that the parents' use of the term "red" is not "arbitrary."

The objection to extreme nominalism, from this point of view, is that if it were true we could never teach anyone else how to use a word, and so could have no common language. For whatever counts as a reason for saying that someone has taught someone else how to use a word also counts as a reason for saying that neither the teacher nor (once he has learned successfully) the pupil is using the term arbitrarily.

There is a connection here with Wittgenstein's argument against the possibility of an essentially private language, i.e., one which it is impossible in principle for the user to teach to anyone else. If to use a term meaningfully is to use it non-arbitrarily, and I can show that I am using it non-arbitrarily only by teaching it to someone else, how can I use a term whose meaning I cannot, in principle, teach to anyone else? The essentially private language, according to Wittgenstein, would be indistinguishable from what the extreme nominalist imagines *our* language to be, and so would not be a language at all. But this is a question which will not be further pursued here.[4]

[4] On the question of "private languages," see Jones, O. R. (ed.), *The Private Language Argument* (London, 1971).

Chapter Five

LOGIC AND ONTOLOGY

We have seen that according to the theories of some philosophers there are universals, whereas according to the theories of others there are not. Furthermore, we have seen that it can be a controversial question whether a given theory implies the existence of universals or not. The Resemblance Theorist offers his theory as a means of avoiding the need for universals, but as we have seen, Russell argues that he is in fact committed to granting the existence of at least one universal, namely resemblance itself.

Universals are not, of course, the only entities whose existence philosophers have disagreed upon. Physical objects are another example, classes yet another, and many more disputed kinds of entities could be mentioned. The problem of universals is thus, in one of its aspects, part of the *ontological problem:* "What kinds of entities are there?"

The ontological problem has in recent times received much attention from writers on logic, the philosophy of logic, and the philosophy of mathematics. As we would expect, these writers consider the problem primarily in relation to theories of the kind found in logic and mathematics.

The relevance of their work to the problem of universals is greater than might be supposed. Sets or classes (the two terms may here be taken as synonymous) play an important part in modern logic and mathematics, and the relation of the concept of "class" to that of "property" is very close.

According to the naïve[1] theory of classes, every non-relational[2] general term has corresponding to it a class, whose members are the things to which the term applies. Thus to the general term "dog" there corresponds the *class of all dogs*. Anything which is a dog is a member of the class of all dogs, and anything which is a member of the class of all dogs is a dog.

There is an obvious analogy here with a possible theory of properties, which would run as follows. Every non-relational general term has corresponding to it a property, which is possessed by just those things to which the term applies. Thus to the general term "dog" there corresponds the *property of being a dog*. Anything which is a dog possesses the property of being a dog, and anything which possesses the property of being a dog is a dog.

Classes themselves may be members of further classes: thus we may speak of the *class of all classes having only two members*, or the *class of all classes all of whose members are dogs*. (The class whose members are my eyes is a member of the first class, the class of all spaniels a member of the second.) But properties, too, can be spoken of as themselves possessing further properties.

For instance, the property of being my nose is possessed by just one thing, so, we might further say, the

[1] Here "naïve" signifies the type of theory current before Russell's paradox (see p. 90) and similar contradictions were discovered.

[2] Relational terms can be treated as corresponding to classes of ordered pairs (see Chapter 4, note 1, above), and these ordered pairs may themselves be identified with certain classes. See, e.g., Halmos, P. R., *Naïve Set Theory* (Princeton, N.J., 1960), sections 6 and 7. As in the previous chapter, I have for the sake of simplicity ignored relational terms.

property of being my nose *possesses the property* of being possessed by just one thing. We notice in this connection that the "general terms" to which classes and properties correspond need not be single words. Any non-relational predicate, whether simple or complex, will serve. It would make no difference if we restricted ourselves to single words, for we could always invent a single word and define it to mean the same as the complex phrase.

So much for the similarities between the concept of class and the concept of property. But there is also an important difference. The identity of classes is determined by their membership: if I liked all my colleagues and nobody else, the class of people I liked would be identical with the class of my colleagues. But the property of being liked by me would not be identical with the property of being my colleague. Rather, we would speak of them as two properties which happen to be possessed by the same things.

In general, if anything which is F is G and anything which is G is F, this is sufficient to make the class of things which are F identical with the class of things which are G, but is not sufficient to make the property of being F identical with the property of being G. What then would be sufficient? The only plausible answer seems to be that the properties would be identical, if it were *necessarily* (or perhaps *analytically*) the case that anything which is F is G and anything which is G is F. For example, we might be willing on these grounds to grant that the property of being a bachelor is the same as the property of being an unmarried man.

For a philosopher such as Quine, who objects to the very concepts of necessity and analyticity, this is a serious objection to any systematic use of the concept of property. And even if we do not share Quine's views on necessity and analyticity, the complications involved in the introduction of modal concepts such as these into a theory will provide a strong reason for using classes rather than properties wherever possible.

From what has been said so far, it seems that, philosophically speaking, properties are like classes, only worse. Any philosophical problems arising about the concept of class may be expected also to arise about the concept of property, while there is one problem about the latter concept, that concerning identity, which is not relevant to the concept of class. Thus any philosophical objections to talk about classes should, it seems, apply a fortiori to talk about properties.

One such objection is raised by Nelson Goodman. Goodman rejects classes on the basis of a methodological principle which he sums up in the slogan "No distinction of entities without distinction of content."

Suppose that we take a number of entities, say x, y, and z, as our starting point. (Goodman calls the entities we start from the "atoms.") Then we may properly go on to speak of further entities consisting of some or all of these atoms taken together.

Thus we may speak of x-together-with-y, x-together-with-z, y-together-with-z, and x-together-with-y-and-z as further entities. These four composite entities are all in Goodman's sense different in content, because no two of them involve exactly the same atoms.

But suppose we now take x-together-with-y and y-together-with-z and put *them* together, calling the resulting entity (x-together-with-y)-together-with-(y-together-with-z). This entity is no different in content from x-together-with-y-and-z, for both involve all three atoms, x, y, and z. Since there is no difference in content between them, they must according to Goodman's principle be the same entity. We thus see that our original four composite entities are all we can get out of x, y, and z. Anything "new" we produce must turn out to be identical with one of these four.

We can now see how classes offend against Goodman's principle. From x, y, and z we can get (among others) the class whose members are x and y, and the class whose members are y and z—we may write these as {x, y} and {y, z} respectively. We may also obtain the class {x, y, z} containing all three atoms. But if we now consider the class whose members are the classes {x, y} and {y, z}, i.e., the class {{x, y}, {y, z}}, it will *not* be identical with {x, y, z}, because although it has, in Goodman's sense, the same content, it does not have the same members. That is, {x, y} is a member of the first class, but not of the second, while x is a member of the second class but not of the first. This is what Goodman calls "the magical process that enables him [the believer in classes] to make two or more distinct entities from exactly the same entities."

The process indeed enables us to "make" infinitely many entities from one entity, or (in many systems of set theory) even from none at all. This is so because, for good technical reasons, set theory allows "unit classes" having only one member, and also an "empty class" with no members at all, usually denoted by "o." Starting from the empty class, we get its unit class {o}, the unit class of this class {{o}}, and so on for as long as we please.

Goodman calls the composite entities which his principle does allow us to speak of as "individual sums." What distinguishes individual sums from classes, as we have seen, is that individual sums which are the same in content are reckoned identical. Goodman's version of nominalism consists essentially in rejecting classes in favor of individual sums. (Goodman's use of the term "nominalism" here is in accord with his extension of the term "universal" to include classes, nominalism being understood as the rejection of universals.)

Goodman does not claim to have proved that his nominalist principle is true. On the contrary, he denies that it can be proved: "The nominalist cannot demonstrate the need for restrictions he imposes on himself." Principles of this kind, he says, "are stipulated as prerequisites of soundness in a philosophic system. They are usually adopted because a philosopher's conscience gives him no choice in the matter."[8]

However, Goodman makes clear that he finds the concept of individual sum intelligible in a sense in which the concept of class is not. Certainly we seem to find no special difficulty in the idea of a thing consisting of several parts (for example, a chess set, or the British Isles). And the concept of individual sum is a far less drastic extension of this idea than the concept of class.

What are the consequences of Goodman's principle for properties? Obviously the idea of a "property theory" on the model of set theory, in which we pass from properties to properties of properties and so on, is ruled out. Indeed, even a system in which we started with entities which were not properties, and laid down that for every predicate applicable to these entities there existed a property, would be ruled out. For suppose the property of being F and the property of being G were properties possessed by exactly the same entities. Then they would not be "distinct as to content," and so according to Goodman's principle ought to be identical. But it is essential to the concept of property that properties do not *have* to be identical under these conditions (though of course they *may* be).

[8] Goodman, N., *The Problem of Universals* (Notre Dame, Indiana, 1956), section 3.

There are no logically compelling reasons for accepting Goodman's principle. But even if we reject it, there is a logically compelling reason for rejecting a "property theory" in which *every* predicate has corresponding to it a property. The same reason compels us to reject also the corresponding version of set theory, in which *every* predicate has corresponding to it a class. This is the contradiction known as "Russell's paradox."

In the case of classes, the paradox is obtained by considering the class of all classes which are *not members of themselves*. (If we object that it makes no sense to speak of a class being a member of itself, we may note that, assuming every predicate to have corresponding to it a class, there must be a class of all classes, and this will be a member of itself.) If we ask whether this class is a member of itself, we find that the hypothesis that it *is* leads to the conclusion that it is *not*, and the hypothesis that it is *not* leads to the conclusion that it *is*. So it is a member of itself if and only if it is not a member of itself, which is absurd. In the case of properties, a similar contradiction is obtained by considering *the property of being a property which does not possess itself*.

The inescapable consequence of these paradoxes is that if we want to construct a theory about classes or about properties, we must start from less sweeping assumptions about the existence of classes and properties respectively. And we are then faced with the question "If only *some* predicates have classes (or properties) corresponding to them, which predicates are they?"

The reader may feel inclined at this point to comment that we do not need Russell's paradox to bring us to the conclusion that not all predicates correspond to properties. Surely nobody ever thought that "being either a white rat or an apple," for example, was a property?

It is of course true that the use of the term "property" outlined at the beginning of this chapter is different from the everyday use of this term. So also is the use of the term "class": we would no more speak in everyday life of "the class of all things which are either white rats or apples" than we would of the corresponding property. Both uses are attempts to generalize and systematize a characteristic feature of the everyday use, namely, the move from saying "This is F" to saying "This has the property of being F" or "This belongs to the class of things which are F." Russell's paradox shows that the desired systematization cannot be achieved as simply as we might have thought.

For a philosopher who attaches importance to that vague intuitive concept of property which inclines us to say that "being either a white rat or an apple" is not a property, the interesting task will be that of making this concept sufficiently precise to enable us to classify all predicates into those which correspond to properties and those which do not. For anyone who attaches more importance to developing a rigorous axiomatic theory of properties (or of classes), the interesting task will be that of modifying the assumptions of the original inconsistent theory in such a way as to render it consistent.

The two tasks are independent. Suppose we arrived at what seemed to be an adequate analysis of the concept of property, by means of which we could classify predicates into "property predicates" and "non-property predicates." We would still not know whether any contradiction could be inferred from the assumption that to every "property predicate" there corresponds a property. On the other hand, a consistent axiomatic theory would not automatically provide us with an analysis of our intuitive concept of property.

An example will make the second point clear. Russell's "theory of types"[4] is an axiomatic theory which may be formulated either in terms of classes or in terms of properties. Let us formulate it in terms of properties. The theory starts by assuming the existence of a number of "individuals"—what these individuals are does not matter, except that they are not properties. There will be various predicates which can be applied only to individuals, and to each such predicate will correspond a property. We may call the individuals entities of type 0, and the properties of individuals entities of type 1. There will also be predicates which can be applied only to properties of individuals, and to these again there will correspond properties, which will be entities of type 3, and so on. Thus a property can be possessed only by entities one type lower than itself: a property of type 1 can be possessed only by individuals, a property of type 2 only by properties of type 1, and so on.

This theory is in fact consistent. (We may note that the Russell paradox, at any rate, cannot be derived since "the property of being a property which does not possess itself," if it existed, would obviously have to be possessed by entities belonging to many different types. So there is no room for it in the theory.) But it does not contribute much to the analysis of our intuitive concept of property. If there are reasons for denying the existence of a property of "being either a white rat

[4] See Russell, *Introduction to Mathematical Philosophy* (London and New York, 1930), or Copi, I. M., *Symbolic Logic* (3rd edition, New York and London, 1967). The theory described in the text is the "simple theory of types." Russell also produced a more elaborate version known as the "ramified" theory, intended to avert certain other paradoxes.

or an apple," we shall not find them in Russell's theory of types.

Of the two tasks I have distinguished, it is naturally that of developing consistent axiomatic theories which has been important in logic and mathematics. The branch of mathematics called "set theory," which deals with classes, has been developed in many directions, and Russell's theory of types is only one of many theories which have been worked out since the discovery of Russell's paradox. (Properties have received much less attention.)

These theories, in common with many other mathematical theories, appear to deal with abstract entities of various kinds. For the philosopher interested in the ontological problem, therefore, two questions suggest themselves: Can these theories be used to prove that the entities they speak of really exist? And if not, do we not need some other way of proving that the required entities exist before we accept the theories as true?

Let us start with the first question. It is obvious that in *some* sense we can use mathematical theories to prove that certain entities exist. In arithmetic we can prove, for example, that there exist infinitely many prime numbers. But "proof" in this sense means showing that, *given certain assumptions,* the conclusion in question can be deduced. In proving that there are infinitely many primes, we *assume* that there are infinitely many natural numbers 1, 2, 3, 4, etc. And this assumption is not itself capable of arithmetical proof.

This does not mean that the basic assumptions of a theory cannot be proved in *another* theory. But the second theory will turn out to have other basic assumptions of its own. For example, systems of set theory have been developed in which the natural numbers are identified with certain classes—one way of doing this is to identify the number 1 with a certain class having only one member, the number 2 with a certain class having two members, and so on.[5] In such a system we can prove that the natural numbers exist. But we cannot prove that classes exist, because the assumption that a certain range of classes exists is one of the basic assumptions of the theory.

It therefore seems that a question like "Do the natural numbers exist?" can only be asked as a mathematical question, as opposed to a philosophical one, if what we really mean is: "Does it follow from the assumptions of such and such a theory that the natural numbers exist?" If the theory in question is arithmetic the answer, trivially, will be yes; if it is a suitable system of set theory it will again be yes, but this time not trivially, since in set theory the existence of numbers is proved rather than simply assumed. Where the question "Do the natural numbers exist?" cannot be understood relative to some particular theory, it cannot be answered by mathematical means. If we say "Yes, I see that it follows from the assumptions of this theory that they exist. But what I want to know is whether they *really* exist, whether the theory is *true*," it seems that we have moved outside the realm of mathematics into that of philosophy.

It might be thought that we have also moved from the realm of meaningful questions to that of meaningless ones. This is the view taken by Rudolf Carnap. According to Carnap,[6] questions of the first type, the "internal questions" ("internal" because we ask them *inside* the framework of a given theory), are meaningful, while questions of the second type, the "external questions," are meaningless.

[5] See Halmos, section 11.

[6] Carnap, R., "Empiricism, Semantics, and Ontology," *Revue Internationale de Philosophie*, XI (1950).

What makes this view plausible is the absence of any recognized method for answering such questions. They cannot be answered by mathematical reasoning, and to say that they are philosophical questions is not to offer an alternative method, for if there is any characteristically philosophical method of giving conclusive answers to questions, it has yet to be discovered.

However, it may be thought that the philosopher who asks "Do numbers exist?" "Do classes exist?" "Do properties exist," etc., and who does *not* mean merely "Do they exist according to such and such a theory?", is not so much uttering empty words as phrasing his question in a misleading way. Perhaps the proper question would be not "Do these entities exist?", but rather "Should we use theories which assume that they exist?"

In the work of Goodman and Quine, we in fact find a tendency to rephrase ontological questions in this way. Goodman in his discussion of classes seems to be arguing that we *ought not to use theories which assume the existence of classes* (or at least, not for purposes of philosophical analysis), rather than that *classes do not exist*.

Likewise, we find Quine saying that statements such as "Numbers exist," or "Classes exist," ought not to be dismissed as meaningless, because "we can have reasons, and essentially scientific reasons" for allowing theories which assume the existence of numbers or classes and for disallowing theories which assume the existence of propositions or attributes (i.e., properties).

Quine goes on to suggest what such reasons might be: "Numbers and classes are favored by the power and facility which they contribute to theoretical physics and other systematic discourse about nature. Propositions and attributes are disfavored by some irregular behavior in connection with identity and substitution. Considerations for and against existence are more broadly systematic, in these philosophical examples, than in the case of rabbits or unicorns or prime numbers between 10 and 20: but I am persuaded that the difference is a matter of degree."[7]

Once the emphasis is put on the theoretical advantages or disadvantages of assuming that certain entities exist, two possibilities suggest themselves: (1) the assumptions which are advantageous in one context might be disadvantageous in another (for example, there might be, as Quine suggests, good reasons for assuming the existence of classes in mathematics and science, and also, as Goodman suggests, good reasons for not assuming it in philosophy), and (2) even in one and the same context, there might be no decisive reasons either for making or for not making a certain assumption, though there were certain advantages and disadvantages in making it, and other, different advantages and disadvantages in not making it.

A possible interpretation of Quine's "difference of degree" might therefore be as follows. At the philosophical end of the scale, we have cases which approximate to types (1) and (2) above. At the other end, we have cases where the considerations for or against making a certain assumption are overwhelmingly on one side (though we may not at any given time know *which* side).

I am supposing, and this is the crucial point, that the difference between the two ends of the scale is *not* merely a function of the state of our knowledge. Thus the retort "But classes (for example) must either exist or not" misses the point, by implying that the considerations for or against assuming the existence of classes must in *fact* be overwhelmingly on one side, though these considerations are unfortunately not available to

[7] Quine, W. V., *Ontological Relativity and Other Essays* (New York, 1969), i, "Existence and Quantification."

us. And to say this is to put the case of classes at the non-philosophical end of the scale. The alternative is to deny that such decisive considerations exist at all.

The formulation and defense of such a view involve many difficulties, which would take us far beyond the scope of this book to explore. But if it is along the right lines at all, it follows that for philosophers to persist in asking "Are there classes?", "Are there numbers?", or "Are there universals?" in the hope of getting a conclusive answer might be a mistake. It might be the case that we cannot hope to show either that we *must* assume the existence of such entities, or that we *must not*.

However, this would not mean that there was nothing further to be said on questions of ontology. The advantages or disadvantages of making any given ontological assumption, and more generally the consequences of making such an assumption, would still need to be considered. And we would still need some account of what it *is* to make an ontological assumption. It is this last question which Quine puts at the center of his discussions of ontology.

In considering this question, Quine is thinking mainly of axiomatic theories;[8] the problem he poses is that of determining the ontological assumptions made by such a theory. The kind of theory Quine has in mind is one based on predicate logic,[9] i.e., one where the theory consists of certain axioms together with all the theorems deducible from these by means of predicate logic.

[8] For an introductory account of axiomatic theories, see Blanché, R., *Axiomatics* (translated by G. B. Keene, New York and London, 1962).

[9] The reader who is unfamiliar with predicate logic will find an elementary account in any modern introduction to logic.

Of such a theory Quine asks, under what conditions should we say that it assumes the existence of entities of such and such a kind? The answer he offers is that the entities whose existence is assumed are those which constitute the *range of the variables of the theory.* (In his paper "On What There Is," Quine summed this up in the slightly misleading slogan "To be is to be the value of a variable.")

To see what this means, let us suppose that we have a set of axioms, formulated using the symbolism of predicate logic and also using other symbols whose meaning is as yet not specified. This Quine would call a "theory form"—it is not as it stands a *theory,* because its axioms are statement forms rather than statements (as "(x) (Fx ⊃ Gx)" is merely a statement form until meanings are specified for F and G).

To get an actual theory, we must *interpret* the theory form. Interpreting it involves, first, specifying a certain range of entities (which are to be the values of the variables). Secondly, any proper names used in the theory form must be interpreted as standing for entities included in this range. And thirdly, any predicate symbols used in the theory must be interpreted as predicates which are significantly applicable to entities in this range.

A formula of the type "(x) (Fx)," or "Everything is F," will then be reckoned *true under that interpretation* if and only if the predicate which is the interpretation of F is true of *all* the specified range of entities. And a formula of the type "(∃x) (Fx)," or "Something is F," will be reckoned true under that interpretation if and only if the predicate which is the interpretation of F is true of *at least one* of the specified range of entities.

Thus "everything" is here understood as meaning *everything in the specified range of entities,* and "something" as meaning *something in the specified range of entities*. This is what is meant by saying that these entities are the *values of the variables*. Theory form and interpretation together constitute the theory. Hence what Quine is saying is that the entities whose existence the theory assumes are those which the interpretation specifies as the range of values of the variables. So, for example, a theory assumes the existence of numbers if and only if numbers are specified as the range of values of the variables.

We may ask, how can numbers be specified as the value of variables unless there *are* numbers? But this is wrong. All we need to do is to present the theory form, and then add the comment: "The variables are to be understood as having numbers as their range of values." Our theory will then be a theory of the kind which, according to Quine, assumes the existence of numbers.

The point may be brought out as follows. Suppose that the theory form contains a predicate symbol N, where Nx is interpreted as meaning "x is a number." Then, if the variables are supposed to have numbers as their range of values, the formula "$(\exists x)$ (Nx)" will obviously be one of those which ought to be true according to the interpretation. Thus what we have is a theory which actually *says* "There are numbers."

But there still seems to be a difficulty. Suppose I am a philosopher who disapproves on principle of assuming the existence of numbers. How am I to express my rejection of such a theory? I cannot say "Actually, your formula '$(\exists x)$ (Nx),' understood as you interpret it, is false," for this would imply that the specified range of values, namely numbers, does not include any numbers.

However, there is an alternative. I can say instead "You *mustn't* specify numbers as the values of your variables," thereby denying the legitimacy or interpreting the theory form in the way intended. The question whether to assume the existence of numbers is thus identified by Quine with the question whether to make use of variables having numbers as their intended range of values.

Some of the implications of this identification are illustrated by Quine's theory of "virtual classes."[10] In this theory, we are allowed the use of symbolic "class names," such as {x: Fx} (normally read "the class of things which are F," or "the class of Fs"). We can use these to say such things as "2 is a member of {x: x is a number}," or "{x: x is divisible by both 2 and 3} = {x: x is divisible by 6}." But these class names are *not* interpreted as standing for entities falling within the range of values of the variables. So from "Fa," where a is a class name, we may not infer "(∃x) (Fx)," and from "(x) (Fx)" we may not infer Fa. Hence, for example, we cannot pass from "2 is a member of {x: x is a number}" to "There is *something* of which 2 is a member."

It may be asked how, if we do not interpret the class names as standing for entities in the range of values of the variables, we *are* to interpret them, since this was described above as the standard procedure for interpreting names. The answer is that we do not interpret them in their own right at all. Instead, we treat sentences containing them as equivalent by definition to other sentences without class names. Thus "2 is a member of {x: x is a number}" is treated as merely another way of saying "2 is a number," and "{x: x is divisible by both 2 and 3} = {x: x is divisible by 6}" as merely another way of saying "what is divisible by both 2 and 3 is divisible by 6, and vice versa."

[10] See Quine, ii.

So the class names, although they behave grammatically like names, are not used *as names;* there is no need of anything in the range of values of the variables for them to stand for. Hence the theory does *not* assume the existence of classes.

If assuming the existence of Xs is to be identified with using variables of which Xs are the intended range of values, we need to ask in turn: What *is* it to use variables in this way? The author of the theory may tell us that the variables are intended to have as their range of values numbers, classes, properties, physical objects, or anything else. But is what he *says* all there is to it? And how are we to know what he means by "number," "class," "property," or "physical object"?

In his recent paper "Ontological Relativity,"[11] Quine takes the view that numbers and classes are "known only by their laws." In other words, what identifies a given theory as being arithmetic, or as being set theory, is the laws which the entities constituting the values of its variables are required to satisfy.

But this raises a problem. Suppose we have a theory which can be recognized as arithmetical by the nature of its laws. What then is the point of going on to say that the entities it assumes are *numbers?* This seems now to amount to saying "The entities this theory assumes are entities which satisfy the laws of this theory," which is an utterly uninformative truism.

We could indeed formulate our arithmetic in some newly invented symbolism, and then proceed to interpret our symbols in terms of the familiar "1, 2, 3, . . . ," "+," "−," etc. Then to say "This theory is about numbers" might be informative to someone who had not noticed that our new symbols could be understood in this way. But the whole operation seems some-

[11] Quine, i, title essay.

what pointless. We might just as well have used the usual symbols from the start.

Suppose, however, that we propose to explain what numbers are by identifying them with certain classes. E.g., we might identify the number 0 with the empty class (let us write the latter $\emptyset$ to distinguish it), the number 1 with the class $\{\emptyset\}$, the number 2 with the class $\{\{\emptyset\}\}$, the number 3 with the class $\{\{\{\emptyset\}\}\}$, and so on. We can then give new meanings to "+," "−," and other such symbols accordingly. This can in fact be done in such a way that all the usual laws of arithmetic become, taken in their new meaning, laws of set theory. That such a reinterpretation of arithmetic in terms of set theory is possible is by no means obvious. So if we now say "This theory is about numbers, and the numbers are $\emptyset$, $\{\emptyset\}$, etc.," this is genuinely informative.

Such considerations lead Quine to formulate what he calls "the principle of ontological relativity," namely, "It makes no sense to say what the objects of a theory are, beyond saying how to interpret or reinterpret that theory in another." In the above examples, our assertion that the theory is about *numbers* was informative only because we were able to explain what we meant by "numbers" in terms of another theory, namely set theory. As long as we had no such second theory to fall back on, the assertion that our theory was about numbers proved uninformative.

The views of Quine which I have attempted to summarize are formulated in terms of axiomatic theories. We need therefore to ask how far they can be applied to other kinds of discourse. In particular, could Quine's criterion for identifying ontological assumptions be used to decide whether our common-sense beliefs about the world involve us in assuming the existence of universals?

At first sight, it may seem that we can quite easily apply the criterion, and show thereby that we do make this assumption. For we do say such things as "They have many qualities in common," "This thing has unusual properties," and so forth. If these statements may be equated with "*There are* many qualities which they have in common" and "*There are* properties which this thing has, and which are unusual" respectively, we seem to have the colloquial equivalent of taking universals as the values of our variables. If we wanted to translate them into logical symbolism, that is, we would need to translate them into the form "$(\exists x)$ (. . .)," where the variable x has universals as its range of values.

But if, still following the analogy between our common-sense beliefs and a theory, we also try to apply Quine's principle of ontological relativity here, the matter becomes more complicated. For according to that principle, the assertion that we are here assuming the existence of universals makes sense only if we can explain *what universals are*, and explain them in terms drawn from outside the area of discourse with which we are concerned.

And indeed, this is borne out by the difficulties run into by a supporter of the Recurrence Theory, who is obliged to fall back on such unhelpful statements as "In the cases where we say two things have a common property, there *really is a common property*," or "When we say the property this thing has is the same as the property that thing has, it *really is the same*." This seems to amount only to pointing out the relevant bits of discourse in a metaphysical tone of voice, and perhaps is vacuous in much the same way that the statements "Arithmetic really is about *numbers*" or "Set theory really is about *classes*" are vacuous.

We might think at this point of turning to the crude

"theory of properties" outlined at the beginning of this chapter for a suitable explanation of what universals are. Then, at least, we can ask a substantial question, namely whether, in the kind of discourse we are considering, we assume the existence of properties in the sense of *entities satisfying the laws of that theory*. If it could be shown that we do, we could then, with the aid of Russell's paradox, draw the interesting conclusion that our common-sense assumptions about properties are inconsistent (as Alfred Tarski[12] has argued, on the basis of a rather similar paradox about truth, that our common-sense beliefs about truth are inconsistent).

But the evidence for our assuming there to be a property corresponding to every predicate is extremely weak. In everyday conversation, we do *not* speak of "the property of being either a white rat or an apple," and if asked whether there is such a property, might well reply that there is not. This is not contradicted by the intuitive obviousness of the schema "A thing is F if and only if it has the property of being F," for this would be adequately explained by supposing that we use "This has the property of being F" as merely another way of saying "This is F," on the model of Quine's "virtual classes." And some everyday talk, such as "This thing has the property of shining in the dark," or "He belongs to the class of people who never admit to a mistake," is surely most naturally interpreted as talk of "virtual properties" and "virtual classes" respectively.

This does not dispose of talk which cannot be explained in this way, as in "They have many qualities in common" or "This thing has unusual properties." But perhaps this talk is best regarded as the first

[12] Tarski, A., "The Semantic Conception of Truth," *Philosophy and Phenomenological Research,* IV (1943–44).

sproutings of an ontological assumption, rather than the full-grown thing. For although we do sometimes talk as if there were properties, we do not seem to take this talk far enough to be committed to any general position as to *what* properties there are. And if we have no such position, we cannot hope to devise a formal theory which corresponds to it.

In any case, how relevant is the question that we assume in everyday discourse as to the dispute between realist and nominalist? Their dispute is surely about whether we need to assume the existence of universals *in philosophy*. According to the realist, this assumption is required to make certain things intelligible, notably the use of general words. According to the nominalist, it is not required; and he may also say, as Goodman would, that its introduction is a positive source of unintelligibility.

If it could be shown that we could not get along without the assumption in everyday discourse (as perhaps we could not get along without the assumption of physical objects), this would support the realist. But this is very dubious. The assumption of properties seems in fact to play a rather small part in everyday discourse. And the nominalist does not need to show that all our property talk can be replaced by non-property talk having exactly the same meaning. He need only show that the consequences of refraining from such talk would not be disastrous.

Chapter Six

SUBJECTS AND PREDICATES

When I say that the cat is hungry, I seem to be doing two things; *referring* to a certain thing, namely the cat, and *saying something about it*, namely, that it is hungry. That which is referred to in asserting a proposition is called the *subject* of the proposition, and that which is said to characterize the subject—in this example, hunger or the state of being hungry—is called the *predicate*. The sentence itself may then be correspondingly divided into two parts, the *subject expression* and the *predicate expression*. Thus in the sentence "The cat is hungry" the subject expression is "the cat" and the predicate expression is "is hungry."

Since Aristotle, most philosophers have supposed a fundamental connection between the subject-predicate distinction and the particular-universal distinction. According to Aristotle, as we have seen, what distinguishes universals from particulars (or "primary substances") is that a universal, unlike a particular, can be "said of" something. In the terminology of subjects and predicates, a universal can be the predicate of a proposition, a particular cannot. Aristotle also held that universals can be "said of" other universals, as when we say that man is a kind of animal. Universals, therefore, can be either subjects or predicates; particulars can only be subjects.

In this chapter we shall be looking at a recent investigation of this line of thought, that undertaken by

P. F. Strawson in the second part of his book *Individuals*.[1] Strawson sets out to examine the subject-predicate and particular-universal distinctions for features which would account for a relation between them of the kind envisaged by Aristotle. Such features are, he concludes, in fact to be found. The theory at which Strawson arrives may, indeed, be regarded as a modern reformulation of Aristotle's theory of universals, which it resembles not only in the fundamental respect just indicated, but in many other respects as well.

Both subject expressions and predicate expressions may, in Strawson's terminology, be spoken of as "introducing" their "terms," which will be, respectively, the subject and the predicate of the asserted proposition. ("Term" for Strawson thus means a thing spoken of, not, as elsewhere in this book, a word or other linguistic expression.) Thus when I assert the proposition that the cat is hungry, the subject expression of my sentence, "the cat," introduces the term *the cat*, and the predicate expression, "is hungry," introduces the term *hunger* or *being hungry*.

Strawson suggests that there is a characteristic difference between the way in which a subject expression introduces its term and the way in which a predicate expression introduces its term. A predicate expression, such as "is hungry," introduces its term in what Strawson calls the "assertive or propositional style," whereas a subject expression does not. If we are given the expression "is hungry" and required to make a sentence from it in the simplest possible way, the result will be a sentence which would normally be used for asserting a proposition, of the form "x is hungry." Other uses of the expression, as in "See whether the cat is hungry"

[1] Strawson, P. F., *Individuals* (London and New York, 1959).

or "If the cat is hungry, give him some food," may be regarded as derived from this basic use.

But a subject expression, such as "the cat" or "Socrates," has no such special connection with the assertion of propositions. "The name 'Socrates' might be completed into *any* kind of remark, not necessarily a proposition; but the expression 'is wise' demands a certain kind of completion, namely completion into a proposition or propositional clause."[2] Subject expressions, too, are what we would use if we were making a list of items, and such listing does not seem to be in any clear sense derived from the assertion of propositions.

Parallel with this account of the subject-predicate distinction Strawson offers an account of the particular-universal distinction, based on the difference which, Strawson suggests, exists between the way in which particulars "collect" universals and the way in which universals "collect" particulars. A particular "collects" all those universals which it exemplifies, whether at some time or other or throughout its existence; a universal "collects" all those particulars which exemplify it, whether at some time or other or throughout their existence. The difference is that the various universals collected by a given particular are linked by way of the continuing identity of the particular, whereas the various particulars collected by a given universal are linked by way of some kind of resemblance. Thus the particular supplies a principle of collection based on continuing identity, the universal a principle of collection based on resemblance.

[2] Strawson, p. 153. T. L. Mei (Mei, T. L., "Chinese Grammar and the Linguistic Movement in Philosophy," *Review of Metaphysics,* XIV (1961) has argued, on the basis of an examination of Chinese grammar, that this aspect of Strawson's theory does not in fact hold good for all languages.

This point is connected with a difference between the conditions in which we say "same particular again" and those in which we say "same universal again." In the first case, the judgment is based on continuing identity, typically involving some sort of spatio-temporal continuity.[3] In the second, it is based on some kind of resemblance. And plainly an entity, whether particular or universal, can supply us with a principle of collection only if we are able to recognize it as the same entity in different circumstances.

The difference between Strawson's two kinds of principle of collection might, perhaps, be brought out as follows. Anyone who has grasped the principle of collection supplied by the universal *red* will be able to recognize occasions for saying "That's red" when they occur. But there is nothing in the principle to lead him from one such occasion to another: knowing the meaning of "red" does not in itself enable me to *locate* examples of redness. Consider in contrast the principle of collection supplied by the particular John, which is, presumably, the principle of personal identity. Given one occasion for saying "That's John," this principle *does* enable me to locate further such occasions, perhaps by following John wherever he goes. On the other hand, it does *not* necessarily enable me to recognize an occasion for saying "That's John" when one occurs. I may fail to recognize John after many years' absence, and my doing so in no way suggests that my grasp of the principle of personal identity must be inadequate.

The above implies that every particular must fall under some general principle for determining the identity of particulars of that kind, as the particular John

[3] There is considerable literature on the question of what the identity of particulars consists. See, e.g., the section headed "Particulars" in Loux, Michael J., *Universals and Particulars* (New York, 1970).

falls under the principle of personal identity. This is in fact Strawson's view. He makes in this connection a distinction between "sortal universals" (corresponding roughly to Aristotle's secondary substances) and "characterizing universals." Sortal universals provide in their own right principles of identity; characterizing universals do this, if at all, only in a derivative way.

Compare, for example, the sortal universal *cat* and the characterizing universal *red*. Anyone who has fully grasped the meaning of "cat" will know both what counts as the same cat again, and where (so to speak) one cat ends and another begins. He will therefore also be able to *count* cats, and hence to answer such questions as "How many cats are now in this room?"

But we cannot in a similar manner say that anyone who has fully grasped the meaning of "red" will know what counts as the same red thing again, or where one red thing ends and another begins, or answer such questions as "How many red things are now in this room?" What counts as the same thing again, where one thing ends and another begins, how many things there are, all depend on what *kind* of things are in question. And to say that a thing is red does not in the required sense tell us what kind it is. The identity of a tomato is not determined in the same way as that of a sunset. Nor is there any answer to the question whether a red rose is *one* red thing or a collection of *many* red things (namely its petals). We can count the roses in a vase or the petals on a rose, but not the "red things" as such.

Red is an example of a characterizing universal which provides no principle of identity at all. Some characterizing universals do, however, supply such principles indirectly. An example of this is the universal *married*. The question "How many married things are now in this room?" does admit of a definite answer, not because *married* supplies a principle of identity in its own right, but because only people can be married, and so the principle of identity supplied by the sortal universal *person* is available for use in this case.

Characterizing universals, according to Strawson, presuppose sortal universals, since characterizing universals are predicated only of particulars whose identity is already determined by means of a principle supplied by some sortal universal. "Characterising universals . . . whilst they supply principles of grouping, even of counting, particulars, supply such principles only for particulars already distinguished, or distinguishable, in accordance with some antecedent principle or method."[4]

It may be asked how the statement that sortal universals supply principles of identity fits together with the earlier statement that it is particulars which supply principles of identity and universals which supply principles of resemblance. However, it is not being claimed that a sortal universal *collects particulars by way of a principle of identity*. On the contrary, it collects them on the basis of the kind of over-all resemblance which exists between one person and another or one cat and another. The principle of identity serves not to *collect* particulars, but to *distinguish* them from one another, and it is on the basis of this same principle that each particular will then itself collect further universals.

We have seen that Strawson explains the subject-predicate distinction by distinguishing between a neutral or "listing" style of term introduction and an "assertive or propositional" style, while he explains the particular-universal distinction by distinguishing between principles of collection based on continuing identity and principles of collection based on resem-

[4] Strawson, p. 168.

blance. But what relation is there between the two distinctions?

It is obvious enough that we very seldom do anything which even looks like predicating a particular. In such cases as "The gesture was Napoleonic," it is possible to say that the term predicated is not the particular Napoleon, but some associated universal, e.g., "having characteristics commonly attributed to Napoleon." And since it is a principle of resemblance (namely, resemblance to Napoleon) which is in question here, the latter account seems preferable. We may note also that to grasp the import of the adjective "Napoleonic," it is not enough to know who Napoleon was: we need also to know, roughly, what he was famous for. This supports what has just been said, for if Napoleon himself were the predicate, knowing who Napoleon was surely *would* be enough.

We may safely claim, then, that the assertive or propositional style characteristic of predicates is not used for introducing particulars. It is, of course, used for introducing universals, which occur as predicates far more often than they do as subjects. But it still remains to be explained how it is that universals do *sometimes* appear as subjects.

The explanation for this, according to Strawson, is that some universals collect other universals in a way analogous to that in which these other universals collect particulars, i.e., on the basis of a principle of resemblance. As an example we may take *species of animal*, which collects *cat, horse, elephant*, etc., in a manner similar to that in which *cat* itself collects particular cats, or *horse* collects particular horses. Since the principle of collection is of the same general kind, it is appropriate to use the same kind of sentence and, just as we would say "Macavity is a cat," say also "The cat is a species of animal."

We may therefore regard as the fundamental type of subject-predicate proposition that in which the subject is a particular and the predicate a universal. But why should this be so?

In answer to this question Strawson offers a new distinction, that between "expressions such that one cannot know what they introduce without knowing (or learning from their use) some distinguishing empirical fact about what they introduce," and "expressions such that one can very well know what they introduce without knowing any distinguishing empirical fact about what they introduce."[5] I shall refer to these, as Strawson does, as "class (1)" and "class (2)" expressions respectively. The distinction between class (1) and class (2) expressions, Strawson suggests, helps to explain why it is appropriate to introduce particulars in the neutral or listing style, and universals in the assertive or propositional style.

Let us see first what Strawson is getting at in distinguishing these two types of expression. We may, reverting to an earlier example, take "the cat" as an example of a class (1) expression, and "is hungry" as an example of a class (2) expression. To know what term is introduced by "is hungry," it is enough for me to understand the meanings of the words. But this is not true of "the cat." When someone says "The cat is hungry," I may fail to understand what term his words "the cat" introduce, not because I don't know what the words "the cat" mean, but because I don't know *which* cat he is referring to on this particular occasion. Likewise (leaving aside the question whether proper names can be said to have meaning), if someone says "John is hungry," I may fail to understand what term the

[5] Strawson, pp. 186–87.

name "John" introduces, because I don't know *which* of the many people named John he has in mind.

To know what term is introduced by a class (1) expression, then, we need, in addition to knowing the meaning (if any)[6] of the expression, to know *which thing the speaker has in mind.* This applies equally to the case where we are ourselves the speaker. I am not introducing a term if I use the expression "the cat" without having any specific cat in mind at all, as I might do to illustrate some point of grammar. Nor do I succeed in introducing a term if I am under some kind of misapprehension, e.g., I intend to refer to *your* cat, but you don't have a cat.

Now if a speaker knows which cat he has in mind when he says "the cat," we can ask him to tell us which cat this is. He can do this either by describing the cat, e.g., as "the black cat which lives next door," or, if the cat in question is actually present, by pointing it out. Things may go wrong at this stage. There may be no black cat living next door, or there may be two and the speaker, not having realized that there were two, is unable to tell us which of the two he meant. Or he might, conceivably, say "That cat over there" and point to a region of space where no cat is to be found. But if nothing goes wrong, it will be the case that he knows an empirical fact in virtue of which he can identify the cat he has in mind—the fact that there is just one black cat living next door, or the fact that there is just one cat in the region of space he indicates. This is what Strawson has in mind when he says that to know what term is introduced by a class (1) expression, one must know a "distinguishing empirical fact" about that thing.

The distinction between class (1) and class (2) ex-

[6] I say "if any" because the expression may be a proper name, and some philosophers have argued that proper names cannot be said to have meaning.

pressions is, according to Strawson, closely related to the distinction between expressions which introduce their terms in the neutral or listing style and expressions which introduce their terms in the assertive or propositional style. The latter are distinguished by a certain incompleteness: an expression like "the cat" is, as it were, more suited to stand on its own than an expression like "is hungry" (and may in fact stand on its own for such purposes as listing or labeling). More specifically, an expression like "is hungry" calls for a certain *kind* of completion, namely completion into a proposition.

This incompleteness, Strawson says, "answers exactly to the failure of this kind of expression to present a fact on its own account. We have a contrast between something which in no sense presents a fact in its own right but is a candidate for being part of a statement of fact, the class (2) expression, and something which does already in a sense present a fact in its own right and is also a candidate for being part of a statement of fact, the class (1) expression. It is appropriate enough that in the explicit assertion constructed by both taken together, it should be the former which carries the propositional symbolism, the symbolism that demands completion into an assertion."

We might think that Strawson is here claiming that a subject expression is always a class (1) expression, and a predicate expression always a class (2) expression. In fact, however, he claims only the second of these things. Subject expressions *can* on occasion be class (2) expressions. An example is "hunger" in the sentence "Hunger drove him to it." For us to know what term is introduced by the word "hunger," it is enough for us to know what the word means. In this respect, the subject expression "hunger" does not differ from the corresponding predicate expression "is hungry."

What then is the relation between the class (1)-class (2) distinction and the particular-universal distinction? Strawson's view is that particulars can be introduced only by class (1) expressions, while universals are normally introduced by class (2) expressions, but may sometimes be introduced by class (1) expressions.

We have therefore the following possibilities:

(a) Subject expression of class (1) introducing a particular (e.g., "the cat").

(b) Predicate expression of class (2) introducing a universal (e.g., "is hungry").

(c) Subject expression of class (2) introducing a universal (e.g., "hunger").

(d) Subject expression of class (1) introducing a universal.

An example of (d) would be "the color this shirt became when I dyed it." Here a universal is identified on the basis of an empirical fact, namely that I dyed the shirt and dyed it to become *one* color (we could not speak of *the* color it became, if I dyed it so as to produce a multi-colored pattern). However, we may note that the universal in question could on another occasion have been introduced by a class (2) expression such as "the color pink" or "the color green." In general, Strawson thinks, a universal is always *capable* of being introduced by a class (2) expression, and indeed by a predicate expression.

The excluded possibilities are:

(e) Subject expression of class (2) introducing a particular.

(f) Predicate expression of class (1) introducing a universal.

(g) Predicate expression of class (1) introducing a particular.

(h) Predicate expression of class (2) introducing a particular.

I have so far outlined Strawson's view in terms of a distinction between particulars and universals. However, Strawson also allows for non-particulars which are not in the traditional sense universals: these would include, for example, classes, numbers, and words (in the sense in which one may speak of different instances of the same word). What he wants to say about these is essentially the same as what he says about universals in the traditional sense.

But there are certain special difficulties here. It is not at first sight clear that classes or words, for example, can be introduced as predicates. When we say "Socrates is a member of the class of men," or "What you see on the blackboard is an instance of the word 'red,'" the predicate, on the face of it, is not the *class*, but *being a member of the class*, not the word, but *being an instance of the word*.

It is relevant at this point to introduce Strawson's concept of a "non-relational tie." Consider the sentence "Socrates is characterized by wisdom." The words "is characterized by" do not, according to Strawson, express a genuine relation between two entities, Socrates and wisdom, but only a "non-relational tie." The objection to regarding them as expressing a genuine relation may be brought out as follows. If, instead of saying "Socrates *is wise*," we may say "Socrates *is characterized by wisdom*," it seems we might also say "Socrates *is characterized by being characterized by wisdom*," "Socrates *is characterized by being characterized by being characterized by wisdom*," and so on ad infinitum.

Now do the infinite series of predicate expressions "is wise," "is characterized by wisdom," etc. all introduce the *same* universal, or does each of them introduce a *different* universal? If the first, we have the seemingly absurd result that, merely in virtue of being wise, Socrates possesses each of an infinite number of properties.[7] But if the second, it surely follows that "being characterized by" is not a genuine relation. For now "Socrates is wise" and "Socrates is characterized by wisdom" have exactly the same meaning, so how can the latter be a relational proposition when the former is not? (A relational proposition always admits of being treated as a simple subject-predicate proposition; we can analyze "John loves Mary" as having *two* subjects, John and Mary, and a relational predicate *loving*, or as having *one* subject and one predicate—either John and *loving Mary*, or Mary and *being loved by John.* The point here is that "Socrates is wise" does not admit of a two-subject analysis at all, and is therefore not a relational proposition.)

The above may remind the reader of the Third Man Argument which we met in connection with Plato, and the resemblance is no accident. It may be argued that Plato's mistake was that of regarding *being characterized by* (in his own terminology, *participating in*) as a genuine relation rather than a non-relational tie, and then, inevitably, found himself unable to explain what manner of relation it was. The difference between regarding *being characterized by* as a genuine relation and regarding it as a non-relational tie is, perhaps, the essential difference between Platonic and Aristotelian realism.

[7] Acceptance of this would raise serious difficulties about the identity of properties. If "being wise" and "being characterized by wisdom" stand for *two* properties, we may wonder how two expressions can ever manage to stand for the *same* property. For the property of being wise and the property of being characterized by wisdom not only are possessed by the same things, but are *necessarily* possessed by the same things. If even this is not enough to make them the same property, what would be?

Let us now return to the two examples of classes and words. It seems entirely reasonable to suppose that the words "is a member of" and "is an instance of" here express non-relational ties. Now "Socrates is characterized by wisdom" can be rewritten in the much less misleading form "Socrates is wise." But how are we similarly to rewrite "Socrates is a member of the class of men" or "What you see on the blackboard is an instance of the word 'red' "? The two examples pose rather different problems, so let us consider them separately.

Our language provides us with subject expressions for introducing words, such as "the word 'red'." But it does not provide us with any predicate expressions other than "is an instance of the word 'red' " and the like, i.e., expressions involving non-relational ties. Strawson says that the project of eliminating talk about "type words" (words conceived of as *having* instances) in favor of talk about token words (words conceived of as *being* instances of words in the first sense) "is apt, except in the bosom of the really fanatical nominalist, to produce nothing but nausea."[8]

However, there is this to be said for the project. If the expression "is an instance of" expresses a non-relational tie, the universal introduced by the expression "is an instance of the word 'red' " ought surely to be capable of being introduced by an expression which does not contain this misleading component. Supposing this to have been done, the sentence "What you see on the blackboard is an instance of the word 'red' " will be replaced by something to the effect "What you see on the blackboard is 'red'-ish," i.e., a sentence which retains the reference to a *token* word ("What you see on the blackboard"), but from which the pre-

[8] Strawson, p. 231.

vious apparent reference to a *type* word ("the word 'red'") is eliminated. Not only nominalism, but Aristotelian realism also, seems to require some such move to be possible.

In the case of classes, the appropriate rewriting seems all too obvious. We can rewrite "Socrates is a member of the class of men" as "Socrates is a man." But the consequences for the concept of class appear somewhat disastrous. On this account, "is a member of the class of men" and "is a man" introduce the *same* entity, which is, presumably, the universal *being a man*. What then does "the class of men" itself introduce? To say that it introduces the *class of men*, an entity different from the universal *being a man*, seems incompatible with regarding "is a member of the class of men" as a mere variant of "is a man." But if we say that it introduces, in a rather odd way, the universal *being a man*, it seems that the *class of men* and the universal *being a man* are one and the same thing. And to accept this would be to abandon the concept of class.

This seems to lend some support to the view of Quine, Goodman, and others who regard set theory as an essentially Platonist activity. Classes, if they are to be anything at all, must be non-particulars which cannot be predicated, and class membership must be a genuine relation. If this is ruled out, classes must be ruled out too. (We may wonder at this point whether Russell's attempt in the "no-class theory" to reduce classes to properties was not, after all, contrary to the opinion of Quine,[9] a reduction in the right direction. What Quine has in mind, I think, is that a Platonist theory of classes is a lesser evil than a Platonist theory of properties. But an Aristotelian theory of properties might still be a lesser evil than either.)

[9] Quine, W. V., *Ontological Relativity and Other Essays* (New York, 1969), p. 101.

Before leaving Strawson, we should take note of an important aspect of his theory which has not as yet been touched on. Strawson does not follow the traditional view that every proposition must have a subject and a predicate (or, in the case of a relational proposition, two or more subjects and a predicate). On the contrary, he suggests that we may regard a language in which there are subject expressions and predicate expressions as something which could, in principle, have developed out of a language in which there is neither. In this language, propositions would be of a kind he calls "feature-placing": propositions to the effect that "There is water here," "There is red here," or even "There is cat here." This is an important departure from the view which regards particulars as the ultimate "given." In Strawson's view, talk of particulars and talk of universals *both* exhibit a logical complexity not present in the hypothetical feature-placing language.

It would be inappropriate to end a book of this kind with "conclusions." Instead, I propose to indicate, with some hesitation, what seem to me some of the most interesting questions arising out of what has been said here. They are as follows:

(1) Is it really the case that one can consistently be a "realist," in the sense of regarding the use of general terms as non-arbitrary, without being a "realist" in the sense of believing in the existence of universals? Could one consistently be a realist in the second sense but not in the first?

(2) The view I have called "extreme nominalism" seems unlikely to be true. But it still seems worth trying to give as clear a formulation of it as possible, if only as a means to classifying the idea of the "non-arbitrariness" of general terms. Is the "non-arbitrariness" of a general term, as the work of Wittgenstein suggests, essentially connected with the need for a language

to be usable by more than one person, and what is the exact nature of the connection?

(3) In Strawson's theory, there seems to be room for further spelling out of why class (1) expressions should be appropriate to that which supplies a "principle of continuing identity," and class (2) expressions to that which supplies a "principle of resemblance." The distinction between locating something and recognizing it seems to be relevant at this point.

(4) Does Strawson's concept of a "non-relational tie" in fact provide us with the means of distinguishing Platonic from Aristotelian realism? The view that it does is in accord with what is usually said about the matter, but seems to require further clarification. Could one, for example, fairly call "Platonic" a way of speaking which essentially involves the use of such expressions as "characterized by"? If so, it becomes a question whether Aristotelian realism can be stated without using Platonic language in the stating of it.

(5) In connection with the above, should Quine's criterion for ontological commitment be regarded as a test for Platonic realism rather than realism as such? Quine and other writers on mathematical logic tend, in fact, to ignore Aristotelian realism as a possible view. Is this because Platonic realism is in fact the only kind of realism to be found embodied in mathematical theories?

(6) If the distinction between Platonic and Aristotelian realism could be made clear, the nominalist would be better placed to decide which of his arguments have force against both varieties of realism and which against only one of them. It seems possible that a sufficiently clear confrontation between nominalism and Aristotelian realism as such has not as yet taken place.

SUGGESTIONS FOR FURTHER READING

Chapter 1

Aaron, R. I., "Porphyry's Problem," in *The Theory of Universals* (Oxford and New York, 1967).

Anscombe, G. E. M., and Geach, P. T., "Aristotle," in *Three Philosophers* (Oxford and New York, 1961).

Aristotle, *Categories* and *De Interpretatione* (translated by J. L. Ackrill, Oxford and New York, 1963), especially pp. 3–11.

Passmore, J., "The Two-Worlds Theory," in *Philosophical Reasoning* (London and New York, 1961).

Plato, *Parmenides* (translated with commentary by F. M. Cornford in *Plato and Parmenides*, London and New York, 1939).

——, *Phaedo*.

Robinson, R., *Plato's Earlier Dialectic* (Oxford and New York, 1950).

Chapter 2

Aaron, R. I., *The Theory of Universals* (New York and London, 1967), Chapters II, III, and IV ("The Character of Locke's Conceptualism," "Berkeley's Criticism," and "Resemblance and Disposition in Hume's Theory").

Berkeley, G., Introduction to *Principles of Human Knowledge* (edited by A. D. Lindsay, London, 1960).

Hume, Introduction to *Treatise on Human Nature* (edited by A. D. Lindsay, London, 1960).

Locke, "Of General Terms," in *An Essay on Human Understanding* (abridged, edited by A. D. Woozley, London and New York, 1964). See also "Of Maxims."

Chapter 3

Aaron, R. I., *The Theory of Universals* (New York and London, 1967), Part II.
Price, H. H., *Thinking and Experience* (London, 1953).
Russell, Bertrand, *Inquiry into Meaning and Truth* (London and New York, 1956), Chapter 25.
——, *Problems of Philosophy* (London and New York, 1912), Chapters 9 and 10.
Woozley, A. D., "Universals," in *Theory of Knowledge* (London and New York, 1949).

Chapter 4

Bambrough, R., "Universals and Family Resemblances," *Proceedings of the Aristotelian Society*, volume LX (1960–61). Also in Loux, M. J. (ed.), *Universals and Particulars* (New York, 1970).
Wittgenstein, L., *Blue and Brown Books* (Oxford and New York, 1958).
——, *Philosophical Investigations* (Oxford and New York, 1963).

Chapter 5

Goodman, N., "A World of Individuals," in *The Problem of Universals* (Notre Dame, Indiana, 1956).
Küng, G., *Ontology and the Logistic Analysis of Language* (Dordrecht, Holland, and New York, 1967).

Quine, W. V., "On What There Is," in *From a Logical Point of View* (Cambridge, Mass., 1953).

——, *Ontological Relativity and Other Essays* (New York, 1969), especially title essay and "Existence and Quantification."

——, *Set Theory and Its Logic* (Cambridge, Mass., 1969).

Chapter 6

Strawson, P. F., *Individuals* (London and New York, 1959), Part II.

——, "Particular and General," *Proceedings of the Aristotelian Society*, volume LIV (1953–54). Also in Loux, M. J. (ed.), *Universals and Particulars* (New Yoik, 1970) and in Strawson, P. F., *Logico-Linguistic Papers* (London, 1971).

BIBLIOGRAPHY

Books and collections

Aaron, R. I., *The Theory of Universals* (2nd ed., Oxford and New York, 1967).

Allan, D. J., *The Philosophy of Aristotle* (Oxford and New York, 1952).

Anscombe, G. E. M., and Geach, P. T., *Three Philosophers* (Oxford and New York, 1961).

Aristotle, *Categories* and *De Interpretatione* (translated by J. L. Ackrill, Oxford and New York, 1963).

Bambrough, R. (ed.), *New Essays on Plato and Aristotle* (London and New York, 1965).

Berkeley, G., Introduction to *Principles of Human Knowledge* (edited by A. D. Lindsay, London and New York, 1960).

Bochenski, J. M., Church, A., and Goodman, N., *The Problem of Universals* (Notre Dame, Indiana, 1956).

Butchkarov, P. K., *Resemblance and Identity* (Bloomington, Indiana, 1966).

Cohen, L. J., *The Diversity of Meaning* (London, 1962).

Crombie, I. M., *An Examination of Plato's Doctrines*, vol. 2 (London and New York, 1963).

Frege, G., *Philosophical Writings* (translated and edited by P. T. Geach and M. Black, Oxford, 1952).

Geach, P. T., *Mental Acts* (London and New York, 1957).

——, *Reference and Generality* (Cornell, New York, 1962).

Goodman, N., *The Structure of Appearance* (Cambridge, Mass., 1951).

Holloway, J., *Language and Intelligence* (London, 1955).

Hume, D., Introduction to *Treatise of Human Nature* (edited by A. D. Lindsay, London and New York, 1960).

Joske, W. D., *Material Objects* (London and New York, 1967).

Kovesi, J., *Moral Notions* (London and New York, 1967), Chapters I, II, and III.

Küng, G., *Ontology and the Logistic Analysis of Language*, (Dordrecht, Holland, and New York, 1967).

Locke, J., *An Essay Concerning Human Understanding* (edited by J. W. Yolton, 2 vols., London, 1961). Abridged editions by A. S. Pringle-Pattison (London and New York, 1924) and A. D. Woozley (London and New York, 1964).

Loux, M. J. (ed.), *Universals and Particulars* (New York, 1970).

Luschei, E. C., *The Logical Systems of Lesniewski* (Amsterdam and New York, 1962).

Passmore, J., *Philosophical Reasoning* (London and New York, 1961).

Plato, *Parmenides*, translated with commentary by F. M. Cornford in *Plato and Parmenides* (London, 1939).

——, *Phaedo*, translated by H. Tredennick in *The Last Days of Socrates* (Baltimore, 1954).

Price, H. H., *Thinking and Experience* (London and New York, 1953).

Quine, W. V., *Word and Object* (Cambridge, Mass., 1960).

——, *Ontological Relativity and Other Essays* (New York, 1969).

——, *Set Theory and Its Logic* (rev. ed.) (Cambridge, Mass., 1969).

Robinson, R., *Plato's Earlier Dialectic* (Oxford and New York, 1950).

Russell, B., *The Problems of Philosophy* (London and New York, 1912).

——, *The Analysis of Matter* (London and New York, 1927).

——, *Introduction to Mathematical Philosophy* (London and New York, 1930).

——, *Inquiry into Meaning and Truth* (London and Baltimore, 1956).

Searle, J. R., *Speech Acts* (Cambridge and New York, 1969).

Shwayder, D. S., *The Modes of Referring and the Problem of Universals* (Berkeley, Calif., 1961).

Stout, G. F., *The Nature of Universals and Propositions* (London, 1921).

Strawson, P. F., *Individuals* (London and New York, 1959).

Wittgenstein, L., *The Blue and Brown Books* (Oxford and New York, 1958).

——, *Philosophical Investigations* (translated by G. E. M. Anscombe, 2nd ed., Oxford and New York, 1963).

Woolhouse, R. S., *Locke's Philosophy of Science and Knowledge* (Oxford and New York, 1971).

Woozley, A. D., *Theory of Knowledge* (London and New York, 1949).

Zabeeh, F., *Universals* (The Hague, 1966).

Articles

Aaron, R. I., "Locke's Theory of Universals," *Proceedings of the Aristotelian Society*, XXXIII (1932–33).

——, "Two Senses of 'Universal'," *Mind*, XLVIII (1939).

——, "Hume's Theory of Universals," *Proceedings of the Aristotelian Society*, XLII (1941–42).

Acton, H. B., "The Theory of Concrete Universals," I, *Mind*, XLV, 9 (1936), II, *Mind*, XLVI (1937).

Aldrich, V. C., "Colors as Universals," *Philosophical Review*, LXI (1952).

Allaire, E. B., "Existence, Independence, and Universals," *Philosophical Review*, LXIX (1960).

Alston, W. P., "Ontological Commitments," *Philosophical Studies* (Minnesota), IX (1958).

Ayer, A. J., "Universals and Particulars," *Proceedings of the Aristotelian Society*, XXXIV (1933–34).

——, "On What There Is," *Aristotelian Society Supplementary Volume* (1951).

Bacon, J., "Ontological Commitment and Free Logic," *Monist*, 53 (1970).

Bambrough, R., "Universals and Family Resemblances," *Proceedings of the Aristotelian Society*, LX (1960–61). Also in Loux, M. J. (ed.), *Universals and Particulars* (New York, 1970).

Baylis, C. A., "Meanings and Their Exemplifications," *Journal of Philosophy*, XXVII (1930).

——, "Universals, Communicable Knowledge, and Metaphysics," *Journal of Philosophy*, XLVIII (1953). Also in Loux, M. J. (ed.), *Universals and Particulars* (New York, 1970).

——, "Logical Subjects and Physical Objects," *Philosophy and Phenomenological Research*, XVII (1957).

Bennett, J., "Substance, Reality and Primary Qualities," *American Philosophical Quarterly*, II (1965).

Bergmann, G., "Particularity and the New Nominalism," *Methodos*, VI (1954).

——, "Strawson's Ontology," *Journal of Philosophy*, LVIII (1961).

Bernays, P., "On Platonism in Mathematics," in Benacerraf and Putnam (eds.), *Philosophy of Mathematics* (Englewood Cliffs, N.J., 1964).

Black, M., "The Elusiveness of Sets," *Review of Metaphysics*, XXIV (1971).

Bochenski, I. M., "The Problem of Universals," in Bochenski, Church, and Goodman, *The Problem of Universals* (Notre Dame, Indiana, 1956).

Braithwaite, R. B., "Universals and the 'Method of Analysis,'" *Aristotelian Society Supplementary Volume*, VI (1926).

Brandt, R. B., "The Languages of Realism and Nominalism," *Philosophy and Phenomenological Research*, XVII (1957).

Brody, B. A., "Natural Kinds and Essences," *Journal of Philosophy*, LXIV (1967).

Butchkarov, P. K., "Concrete Entities and Concrete Relations," *Review of Metaphysics*, X (1957).

Campbell, K., "Family Resemblance Predicates," *American Philosophical Quarterly*, II (1965).

Carmichael, P., "'Derivation' of Universals," *Philosophy and Phenomenological Research*, VIII (1948).

Carnap, R., "Empiricism, Semantics, and Ontology," *Revue Internationale de Philosophie*, XI (1950).

——, "The Methodological Character of Theoretical Concepts," *Minnesota Studies in the Philosophy of Science*, I (Minneapolis, 1956).

Chomsky, N., and Scheffler, I., "What Is Said to Be," *Proceedings of the Aristotelian Society*, LIX (1958–59).

Church, A., "Propositions and Sentences," in *The Problem of Universals* (Notre Dame, Indiana, 1956).

——, "Ontological Commitment," *Journal of Philosophy*, 55 (1963).

Cooper, N., "Ontological Commitment," *Monist*, 50 (1966).

Cornman, J. W., "Language and Ontology," *Australasian Journal of Psychology and Philosophy*, XLI (1963).

Darrant, M., "Feature Universals and Sortal Universals," *Analysis*, 139 (1970).

Dawes-Hicks, G., "Are the Characteristics of Particular Things Universal or Particular?", *Aristotelian Society Supplementary Volume*, III (1923).

Donagan, A., "Universals and Metaphysical Realism," *Monist*, Vol. 47, No. 2 (1963). Also in Loux, M. J. (ed.), op. cit.

Ducasse, C. J., "Some Critical Comments on a Nominalistic Analysis of Resemblance," *Philosophical Review*, XLIX (1940).

Dummett, M., "Nominalism," *Philosophical Review*, LXV (1940).

——, "Truth," *Proceedings of the Aristotelian Society*, LIX (1950).

Duncan-Jones, A. E., "Universals and Particulars," *Proceedings of the Aristotelian Society*, XXXIV (1933–34).

Emmett, E. R., "Philosophy of Resemblances," *Philosophy*, XXXIX (1954).

Ewing, A. C., "The Problem of Universals," *Philosophical Quarterly*, 21, No. 84 (1971).

Frege, G., "Concept and Object," translated in *Philosophical Writings*, edited by P. T. Geach and M. Black (Oxford, 1952).

Furlong, E. J., Mace, C. A., and O'Connor, D. J., "Abstract Ideas and Images," *Aristotelian Society Supplementary Volume*, XXVII (1953).

Gasking, D., "Clusters," *Australasian Journal of Psychology and Philosophy*, XXXVIII (1960).

Geach, P. T., "On What There Is," *Aristotelian Society Supplementary Volume* (1951).

——, "What Actually Exists," *Aristotelian Society Supplementary Volume*, XLII (1968).

Ginascol, F. H., "The Question of Universals and the Problem of Faith and Reason," *Philosophical Quarterly*, IX (1959).

Goddard, L., "Predicates, Relations and Categories," *Australasian Journal of Psychology and Philosophy*, XLIV (1966).

Goodman, N., "A World of Individuals," in *The Problem of Universals* (Notre Dame, Indiana, 1956).

——, "On Relations That Generate," *Philosophical Studies*, 9, (1958). Also in Benacerraf and Putnam (eds.), *Philosophy of Mathematics* (Englewood Cliffs, N.J., 1964).

Goodman, N., and Quine, W. V., "Steps Towards a Constructive Nominalism," *Journal of Symbolic Logic*, XII (1947).

Haack, R. J., "Natural and Arbitrary Classes," *Australasian Journal of Philosophy*, XLVII (1969).

Hacking, I., "A Language Without Particulars," *Mind*, LXXVII (1968).

Hartshorne, C., "Are There Absolutely Specific Universals?", *Journal of Philosophy*, LXVIII, No. 3 (1971).

Hintikka, J., "Existential Presuppositions and Existential Commitments," *Journal of Philosophy*, 56 (1959).

Jones, J. R., "Are the Qualities of Particular Things Universal or Particular?", *Philosophical Review*, LVIII (1949).

——, "What Do We Mean by an 'Instance,'" *Analysis*, XI (1950).

——, "Characters and Resemblance," *Philosophical Review*, LX (1951).

Joseph, H. W., "Universals and the 'Method of Analysis,'" *Aristotelian Society Supplementary Volume* (1926).

Kearns, J. T., "Sameness and Similarity," discussion with B. Blanshard, *Philosophy and Phenomenological Research*, 29 (1969).

Khatchadourian, H., "Common Names and 'Family Resemblances,'" *Philosophy and Phenomenological Research*, XVIII (1958).

——, "Natural Objects and Common Names," *Methodos*, XIII (1961).

Klemke, E. A., "Universals and Particulars in a Phenomenalist Ontology," *Philosophy of Science*, XXVII (1960).

Knight, H., "A Note on the 'Problem of Universals,'" *Analysis*, I (1933).

Knight, T. A., "Questions and Universals," *Philosophy and Phenomenological Research*, XXVII (1966).

Körner, S., "On Determinables and Resemblances," *Aristotelian Society Supplementary Volume*, XXXIII (1959).

Kultgen, J. H., "Universals, Particulars, and Change," *Review of Metaphysics*, IX (1956).

Lazerowitz, M., "The Existence of Universals," *Mind*, LV (1946).

Leonard, H. S., "Essences, Attributes and Predicates," *Proceedings and Addresses of the American Philosophical Association*, 37 (1964).

Lloyd, A. C., "On Arguments for Real Universals," *Analysis*, XI (1951).

Lomasky, L., "Nominalism, Replication and Nelson Goodman," *Analysis*, 29 (1968–69).

Long, P., "Are Predicates and Relational Expressions Incomplete?", *Philosophical Review*, LXXVIII (1969).

Loux, M. J., "The Problem of Universals," in Loux, M. J. (ed.), *Universals and Particulars* (New York, 1970).

Manser, A. R., "Games and Family Resemblances," *Philosophy* (1967).

Margolis, J., "Some Ontological Policies," *Monist*, 53 (1970).

McCloskey, H. J., "The Philosophy of Linguistic Analysis and the Problem of Universals," *Philosophy and Phenomenological Research*, XXIV (1964).

Mei, T. L., "Chinese Grammar and the Linguistic Movement in Philosophy," *Review of Metaphysics*, XIV, No. 3 (1961).

——, "Subject and Predicate: A Grammatical Preliminary," *Philosophical Review* (1961).

Moore, G. E., "Are the Characteristics of Particular Things

Universal or Particular?", *Aristotelian Society Supplementary Volume*, III (1923).

Moravscik, J., "Strawson on Ontological Priority," in *Analytical Philosophy* (edited by R. J. Butler, Oxford and New York, 1965).

O'Connor, D. J., "On Resemblance," *Proceedings of the Aristotelian Society*, XLVI (1945–46).

——, "Stout's Theory of Universals," *Australasian Journal for Psychology and Philosophy*, XXVII (1949).

——, "Names and Universals," *Proceedings of the Aristotelian Society*, LIII (1952–53).

O'Shaughnessy, R. J., "On Having Something in Common," *Mind*, LXXIX, No. 315 (1970).

Pap, A., "Nominalism, Empiricism, and Universals," I, *Philosophical Quarterly*, IX (1959), II, *Philosophical Quarterly*, X (1960).

Parsons, C., "Ontology and Mathematics," *Philosophical Review*, LXXX (1971).

Parsons, T., "Ontological Commitment," *Journal of Philosophy*, 64 (1967).

——, "Criticism of 'Are Predicates and Relational Expressions Incomplete?' ", *Philosophical Review*, LXXIX (1970).

Pears, D. F., "Universals," *Philosophical Quarterly*, I (1951). Also in Loux, M. J. (ed.), *Universals and Particulars*, (New York, 1970).

——, "A Critical Study of P. F. Strawson's *Individuals*," I, II, *Philosophical Quarterly*, XI (1961).

Phillips, E. D., "On Instances," *Analysis*, I (1934).

Pompa, L., "Family Resemblances," *Philosophical Quarterly*, XVII (1967).

Prior, A. N., "Determinables, Determinates, and Determinants," I, II, *Mind*, LVIII (1949).

Quine, W. V., "On Universals," *Journal of Symbolic Logic*, XII (1947).

——, "On Carnap's Views on Ontology," *Philosophical Studies*, 2 (1951).

——, "Ontology and Ideology," *Philosophical Studies*, 2 (1951).

——, "On What There Is," *Aristotelian Society Supple-*

mentary Volume (1951). Also in Quine, W. V., *From a Logical Point of View* (Cambridge, Mass., 1953).

——, "A Logistical Approach to the Ontological Problem," in Quine, W. V., *The Ways of Paradox* (New York, 1966).

——, "Russell's Ontological Development," *Journal of Philosophy*, 63 (1966).

Quine, W. V., and Goodman, N., "Steps Towards a Constructive Nominalism," *Journal of Symbolic Logic*, XII (1947).

Quinton, A., "Properties and Classes," *Proceedings of the Aristotelian Society*, LVIII (1957–58).

Ramsey, F. P., "Universals and the 'Method of Analysis,'" *Aristotelian Society Supplementary Volume*, VI (1926).

——, "Universals," in Ramsey, F. P., *Foundations of Mathematics* (New York, 1931).

Rankin, K. W., "The Duplicity of Plato's Third Man," *Mind*, LXXVIII (1969).

——, "Is the Third Man Argument an Inconsistent Trial?", *Philosophical Quarterly*, 20, No. 81 (1970).

Raphael, D. D., "Universals, Resemblance, and Identity," *Proceedings of the Aristotelian Society*, LV (1954–55).

Roma, E., and Thomas, S. B., "Nominalism and the Distinguishable Is Separable Principle," *Philosophy and Phenomenological Research*, XXVIII (1968).

Russell, B., "On the Relations of Universals and Particulars," *Proceedings of the Aristotelian Society*, XII (1911–12).

Ryle, G., "Systematically Misleading Expressions," *Proceedings of the Aristotelian Society*, XXXII (1931–32).

Sachs, D., "Does Aristotle Have a Doctrine of Secondary Substances?", *Mind*, LVIII (1948).

Scheffler, I., and Chomsky, N., "What Is Said to Be," *Proceedings of the Aristotelian Society*, LIX (1958–59).

Searle, J. R., "On Determinables and Resemblance," *Aristotelian Society Supplementary Volume* (1959).

Sellars, W., "Logical Subjects and Physical Objects," *Philosophy and Phenomenological Research*, XVII (1957).

——, "Grammar and Existence: A Preface to Ontology," *Mind*, LXIX (1960).

——, "Abstract Entities," *Review of Metaphysics*, XVI (1963).

Simon, M. A., "When Is a Resemblance a Family Resemblance?", *Mind*, LXXVIII (1969).

Sinisi, V. F., "Nominalism and Common Names," *Philosophical Review*, LXXI (1962).

Smith, N. K., "The Nature of Universals," I, II, III, *Mind*, XXXVI (1927).

Sommers, F., "Types and Ontology," *Philosophical Review*, 72 (1963). Also in Strawson, P. F. (ed.), *Philosophical Logic* (Oxford and New York, 1967).

Stoothoff, R. H., "What Actually Exists," *Aristotelian Society Supplementary Volume*, XLII (1968).

Stout, G. F., "Things, Predicates, and Relations," *Australasian Journal of Psychology and Philosophy*, XVIII (1940).

——, "Are the Characteristics of Particular Things Universal or Particular?", *Aristotelian Society Supplementary Volume*, XLII (1968).

Strawson, P. F., "Particular and General," *Proceedings of the Aristotelian Society*, LIV (1953–54). Also in Loux, M. J. (ed.), *Universals and Particulars* (New York, 1970), and Strawson, P. F., *Logico-Linguistic Papers* (London, 1971).

——, "Singular Terms and Predication," *Journal of Philosophy*, 58 (1961).

——, "The Asymmetry of Subjects and Predicates," in *Language, Belief and Metaphysics* (Vol. I of *Contemporary Philosophic Thought*, edited by H. E. Kiefer and M. K. Munitz, New York, 1970), and P. F. Strawson, *Logico-Linguistic Papers* (London, 1971).

Stroll, A., "Meaning, Referring and the Problem of Universals," *Inquiry*, IV (1961).

Taylor, C. C. W., "Forms as Causes in the *Phaedo*," *Mind*, LXXVIII (1969).

Teichmann, J., "Universals and Common Properties," *Analysis*, 29 (1968–69).

Thomas, W. J., "Platonism and the Skolem Paradox," *Analysis*, 28 (1967–68).

Thompson, M. H., "Abstract Entities," *Philosophical Review*, LXIX (1960).

——, "Abstract Entities and Universals," *Mind*, LXXIV (1965).

Toms, E., "Non-Existence and Universals," *Philosophical Quarterly*, VI (1956).

Urmson, J. O., "Recognition," *Proceedings of the Aristotelian Society*, LVI (1955–56).

Vision, G., "Searle on the Nature of Universals," *Analysis*, New Series No. 137 (1970).

Wallace, J. R., "Sortal Predicates and Quantification," *Journal of Philosophy*, LXII (1965).

Welker, D. D., "Linguistic Nominalism," *Mind*, LXXIX No. 316 (1970).

Wolterstorff, N., "Are Properties Meanings?", *Journal of Philosophy*, LVII (1960).

——, "Qualities," *Philosophical Review*, LXIX (1960). Also in Loux, M. J. (ed.), *Universals and Particulars* (New York, 1970).

——, "On the Nature of Universals," in Loux, M. J. (ed.), *Universals and Particulars* (New York, 1970).

Woodger, J. H., "Science Without Properties," *British Journal for the Philosophy of Science*, 2 (1952).

Woozley, A. D., "Universals," *Encyclopaedia of Philosophy*, VIII, pp. 194–206.

INDEX

(References to persons in the notes or bibliography are not included.)

Aaron, R. I., 55–58, 66
Abstraction, 32–36, 39
Anti-realism, ix–x, 26, 27, 53, 67
Aristotle, 1, 7–17, 20–22, 25, 30, 37, 106–7, 110
Axiomatic theories, 92–95, 97–102

Bambrough, R., 73–74, 77
Berkeley, 28, 32, 37, 38–42, 43, 45–50

Carnap, R., 94
Characterizing universals, 110
Classes, viii, 85–97, 100–3, 116–20
  virtual, 100, 104
Classification, x, 14–15, 20, 37–38
Conceptualism, 26–27

Definition, 1–2, 3, 4, 7, 11, 14, 20
  "ostensive definition," 72–73, 75

Feature-placing propositions, 121
Forms, 1–8, 10–11, 15–17, 22–26, 75, 77

General terms, viii, 7, 16–21, 24, 26–27, 28, 31–32, 43–52 *passim*, 53–67 *passim*, 85–86
  "Arbitrariness" or "non-arbitrariness" of, viii, 26–27, 53, 67, 68, 72–73, 82, 121
Goodman, N., 87–90, 95, 96, 105, 120

Hume, 28, 31, 37, 42–44, 46, 48–51

Ideas, 1–3, 29–43, 45–50
  general, 31–37, 38, 41, 42, 48
Identity, principles of, 108–11, 122
Images, 37, 38, 39–40, 46–52

Imitation, 5, 10, 22–24
Individual sums, 88–89
"Introduction of terms," 107, 111–17

Locke, 28, 29, 31–38, 39–40, 45, 46, 48
Logic, viii, 84, 93, 97, 122

Mathematics, viii, 4, 84, 93–96, 101–3, 122

Names, 100
  proper, 113, 114 note 6
Nominalism, 26–27, 74, 88, 105, 120, 122
  "extreme nominalism," 26, 68, 81, 82, 121
Numbers, viii, 94–96, 99–103, 117

Ontology, vii, 84, 93, 97, 102–5

Participation, 4, 7, 22–24, 75, 77, 118
Plato, ix, 1–7, 8–12, 15–26, 75, 77, 118
Properties, vii, 53–60 *passim*, 75–78, 85–87, 89–92, 101–5 *passim*, 118, 120
  identity of, 86, 89, 96, 109, 118 note 7

Quantifiers, 99–100, 103
Quine, W. V., 86, 95–100, 101–2, 120, 122

Realism, viii, ix, 15–26, 53, 67, 74–75, 77, 105, 121–22
  Platonic and Aristotelian, 15–26, 118, 120, 122
Recurrence Theory, 54–55, 57–59, 67, 72–75, 77, 103
Relations, vii, 53–54, 61, 68 note 1, 85 note 2, 117–19, 120
  "connecting relation," 76–78, 80
  and "non-relational ties," 117–20, 122
Reminiscence, 6, 6 note 1
Resemblance, viii, 23, 35, 37, 42, 45, 53–67 *passim*, 72, 76, 80, 108, 111–12
  Resemblance Theory, 53–54, 56–57, 60–67, 72–75, 77, 84
  exact resemblance, 54–58, 57 note 2, 79–80
  family resemblances, 74, 80
  principles of resemblance, 108, 111–12, 122
Russell, B., ix, 60–62, 65–66, 84, 92, 120
  Russell's paradox, 90, 91, 93, 104

Sets, *see* Classes.
Socrates, 1–2
Sortal universals, 110–11
"Standard particular," 54, 61–64
Strawson, P. F., 107–11, 112–19, 121–22
Subject and predicate, 106, 108, 111, 113, 121

Subject and predicate (*cont'd*)
subject expression and predicate expression, 106–7, 114–17, 119, 121
Substances, 9–15
primary and secondary, 13–14, 106, 110

Tarski, A., 104
"Third Man Argument," 23, 23 note 2, 118
Types, theory of, 92–93, 92 note 4

Vagueness, 59–60
Variables, range of, 98–103

Wittgenstein, L., 73–75, 77–81, 82–83, 121
Words (as non-particulars), 44–45, 45 note 7, 117–19